STOP CHASING EASY

STEPHEN BLANDINO

Foreword by Scott Wilson

Stop Chasing Easy
Pursuing a Life That Counts Today...and For Eternity
www.stephenblandino.com
www.stopchasingeasy.com

Copyright © 2022 by Stephen Blandino

Published by The Core Media Group, Inc.
P.O. Box 2037, Indian Trail, NC 28079
www.thecoremediagroup.com

Published in association with the literary agency of WordServe Literary Group, Ltd.,
www.wordserveliterary.com

Cover Design: Stephen Blandino
Interior Design: Nadia Guy
Cover photo provided by Eoneren/Getty Images

ISBN 978-1-950465-47-7

To Karen,
Together we're pursuing a life
that counts today...and for eternity.
I love you forever.

Praise For
Stop Chasing Easy

"Life is getting harder. At least for me. I thought it would get easier, but it's not. It is getting harder because I have larger vision, greater influence, and more passion than ever. I'm guessing the same is true for you. In his latest book, *Stop Chasing Easy*, my good friend Stephen Blandino reminds us why *easy* isn't fruitful and *hard* isn't to be avoided. You'll read, learn, grow, and share with all your friends—go hard!"
-Dr. Sam Chand, Leadership Coach, Consultant, and Author of *Leadership Pain* and *Bigger, Faster Leadership*

"Stephen Blandino's new book, *Stop Chasing Easy*, is both candid and compelling. It will reset your priorities and inspire you to greater service. If you want to see the challenges of life from a different perspective, this is a must-read."
-Hal Donaldson, CEO & President, Convoy of Hope, and Author of *Disruptive Compassion: Becoming the Revolutionary You Were Born to Be*

"Practical. Inspiring. Challenging. In *Stop Chasing Easy* Stephen has once again laid out a challenge to live a life that counts. Everyone can benefit from his well thought out process."
-Darius Johnston, Lead Pastor, Movement City Church, Fort Worth, TX

"In *Stop Chasing Easy*, Stephen Blandino has given us a fresh, practical, inspirational and biblical perspective on how to live a fulfilling life that matters for eternity."
-Steve Moore, President, Nexleader, and Author of *The Top 10 Leadership Conversations in the Bible*

"Stephen Blandino has written another gem! What a helpful and incredibly inspiring work on how to chase our God-given assignments without taking all the shortcuts our culture offers. A must read for anyone who wants to get to where we are going — God's way!"
-Blaine Bartel, Speaker, Coach, and Author of *Death by a Thousand Lies*

"Stephen Blandino's latest book, *Stop Chasing Easy*, is a practical call to all Christ followers about a true "road less traveled." Stephen's highly applicable insights map the journey for us to pursue making Jesus famous, even over ourselves. This approachable book is a must read for anyone on the journey of faith, reminding both veterans and beginners of what it means to follow Jesus in both the good and bad times of life and ministry."
-Dr. Aaron Cole, Senior Pastor, Life Church, Wisconsin, and Chairman of the Board at Convoy of Hope

"Stephen's writing is always practical and he's such a great storyteller! As his lifelong friend, I can tell you that he writes what he lives. *Stop Chasing Easy* is valuable wisdom born from scripture and Stephen's daily life as a pastor, husband, dad, and follower of Jesus."
-Jeff Galley, Central Group Leader, LifeGroups and Missions, Life Church

"Why do most organizations stop growing? They choose to. They choose not to make the courageous decisions they need to make and have the courageous conversations they need to have! Stephen has never tried to take the easy way out. He chooses courage and hard work, and it has paid off. This book is a look into his soul...and yours, and unlocks the pathway toward progress for your ministry or organization!"
-Shawn Lovejoy, Founder and CEO of Courage to Lead and Author of *Measuring Success*

"Stephen Blandino is a profound thinker and a prolific writer who writes from a place of wisdom and humility. As an author, he possesses the rare ability to take complex concepts, unpack them in language that can be understood by all, and offer very clear application for his readers. In *Stop Chasing Easy*, Stephen provokes the reader to consider a paradigm shift, to embrace a counter cultural mindset. While our contemporary society emphasizes the pursuit of easy, we are challenged to do hard things that matter. This book will inspire and equip you with the Biblical principles and practical steps to achieve God's will for your life and to do something that echoes in eternity."
-Ben Sterciuc, Entrepreneur, Professor, and Founder of Vital Solutions

"American Christians too often want to live on safe, comfortable Easy Street. In *Stop Chasing Easy*, however, Stephen Blandino argues that that Easy Street is really a dead end. Drawing on Paul's letter to the Philippians, Blandino shows that God wants Christians to travel the path from pessimism to perspective, from comfort to character, from the temporal to the eternal, and from looking back to moving forward with the gospel. *Stop Chasing Easy* is an action plan for Christians who want to live a life that makes a difference."
-George P. Wood, Executive Editor, *Influence Magazine*

"I like being around people who do hard things. Probably because I want my life, and those closest to me to be marked by bold obedience and courageous actions. In *Stop Chasing Easy*, Stephen Blandino invites us to follow Jesus in ways where we opt into hard things rather than out of them. He presents four trades that will transform our faith and leave an eternity shaping wake."
-Jeffery Portmann, Director, Church Multiplication Network

"Right now we have an epidemic of leaders looking for a way out. Some are so desperate for Easy Street, they self-sabotage. This book is a charge against that, and shows us the noble pursuit of what matters most on this side of eternity. Stephen is someone who challenges and inspires my faith, and in *Stop Chasing Easy* he's done it yet again. Highly encourage leaders and pastors to get your hands on this book!"
-Kurtis Parks, Songwriter and Lead Pastor, Bridges Nashville

Stop Chasing Easy made me realize that my mindset was set on comfort. A confession I wish I never had to make, but one that we so easily fall into. Stephen Blandino did it again! This book was like a conversation about my purpose, and now I have to change my entire perspective. *Stop Chasing Easy* is a brilliant read filled with stories that will steer you towards making a greater difference than you thought was possible! The only thing wrong with this book is that I wish I had read it 15 years ago!

-Preston Ulmer, Author and Founder of The Doubters' Club

Table of Contents

Foreword

One thing I've learned about life and leadership is that the most significant dreams are never easy to obtain. They always come with a price, and you can't take short-cuts to get to your goal. And yet, regardless of how inspiring our dreams might be, culture has a way of enticing us to pursue Easy Street instead.

Easy Street represents a life of ease, comfort, and convenience. It avoids anything hard, and as a result, accomplishes nothing great. While on the surface Easy Street sounds enticing, the apostle Paul makes it clear: "Easy street is a dead-end street."

In *Stop Chasing Easy*, Stephen Blandino offers us a better path forward. He takes us on a powerful journey through the book of Philippians where the apostle Paul confronts Easy Street and presents us with four important trade-offs to make our lives truly count.

Stephen begins with the first trade off—our *mindset*—by challenging us to trade pessimism for perspective. Having the right perspective helps us respond to challenges in a way that maximizes our growth and impact. Then he tackles the importance of *maturity* where we learn to trade comfort for character. As our character matures, God is able to trust us with greater responsibility and expanded opportunity.

Next, Stephen calls us to embrace a *mission* where we trade the temporal for the eternal. Rather than chasing empty success, he inspires us to pursue a mission that matters today and for eternity. Finally, Stephen equips us for *movement* as we trade regression for progression.

Rather than returning to the comforts of Easy Street, we discover the keys to keep moving forward with the mission God has called us to pursue.

Stephen not only challenges us to reject the empty lies of Easy Street, but he equips us with the strategies to get from where we are to where God wants us to go. *Stop Chasing Easy* is filled with inspiring stories, rich biblical insight, and practical application.

I've known Stephen Blandino for thirty years, and I've watched him practice the principles he teaches in *Stop Chasing Easy*. He has an unwavering commitment to personal growth, and his insights on leadership and purpose will inspire you to reach your full potential.

Don't waste your time chasing Easy Street. In the end, it will only disappoint you and leave you with a lifetime of regrets. Instead, catch a vision for a mission bigger than yourself, and discover how to make your life count today—and for eternity.

-Scott Wilson, CEO of 415 Leaders and RSG Leaders, Global Pastor of Oaks Church, and Author of *Impact: Releasing the Power of Influence*

Introduction

N obody hits the gas when they're *knowingly* driving down a dead-end street. Especially at night, in the rain, when it's foggy. Doing so is a recipe for disaster. Even if the sun is up and the sky is clear, most of us avoid dead-end streets. They get you nowhere fast and you inevitably back-track, losing precious time.

But that's rarely our problem.

Unknowingly driving down dead-end streets is our *real* problem.

Dead-end streets show up in the most unexpected places. We spend money like there's no tomorrow, crashing into a dead-end street called bankruptcy. We race down the road of safety and security, only to find ourselves in a dead-end job. We hit the gas, driving as fast as we can toward success, only to end up in a ditch after we discover our definition of success is misguided. The examples are endless.

But there's one dead-end street that we're so convinced is good (even great), that we dream of building a home, raising our kids, and pursuing our futures nestled in its promise of perfection. You and I know this enticing street as "Easy Street."

All of us long for Easy Street. It's paved with comfort and lined with safety. It travels through the trouble-free hills of security, and its road signs point to a pain-free destination where blessings abound. Who wouldn't want to live on Easy Street? Who wouldn't want their friends and family to travel with them down a road of painless prosperity? After all, Easy Street is what many of us dream of, long for, and spend our lives pursuing. It's the good life we were always told to chase when we were growing up. And it seems like a logical, wonderful pursuit… until it turns out that Easy Street is a dead-end street.

The things we enjoy on easy street are not inherently wrong. I'm not saying that blessings are bad or that the comforts of life are evil, and I'm not suggesting that we should intentionally make things harder than they need to be. The goal in life is not to accumulate a trophy case full of pain, suffering, and hardship. What I am saying is that the pursuit of Easy Street doesn't satisfy. In the end, it leaves you empty and deceives you into believing that the purpose of life is to avoid anything difficult. Nobody remembers those who parked their lives on Easy Street. Their names drift into oblivion.

The people you and I remember, admire, and celebrate are those who invested their lives in pursuit of a noble mission. The people we uphold as heroes are the men and women who endured hardship, overcame great odds, and marched boldly into a future of significance. Yet while these are the names we remember, we often forget the price they had to pay and the fears and uncertainties they had to face.

For example, we remember the victory of David slaying goliath, but we forget the hardship of betrayal as he ran for his life from King Saul. We remember the stunning 52-day leadership feat where Nehemiah rallied the Israelites to rebuild the wall around Jerusalem, but we forget the unrelenting ridicule he experienced along the way. We remember the magnitude of the apostle Paul's missionary journeys, divine miracles, and life-giving letters found in the New Testament, but we forget the hardship he faced when he was beaten, shipwrecked, and imprisoned. For each one of these heroes, faith flourished in the halls of hardship.

A life that counts today—and for eternity—isn't a matter of being famous or well-known. Avoiding Easy Street doesn't guarantee your life will be written about in books or celebrated at conferences. In fact, most legacies are draped in shades of anonymity. But that doesn't mean their life counts any less. You can be faithful without being famous. You can be a legacy-maker without being renowned in your field of work. Your legacy begins when you stop chasing easy.

The greatest victories of life are not won on Easy Street; they're won on the road that weaves through the mountains of resistance, the valleys of suffering, and the deserts of hardship. Everybody longs for significance, but few are willing to travel its winding path. We would rather relax on Easy Street and simultaneously experience the reward of a disciplined life. That cozy duo doesn't exist.

Interestingly, we get a frank look at Easy Street in a New Testament letter written by the apostle Paul around A.D. 62 to the church in the city of Philippi. The opening verse begins, "This letter is from Paul and Timothy, slaves of Christ Jesus. I am writing to all of God's holy people in Philippi who belong to Christ Jesus, including the church leaders and deacons" (Philippians 1:1). Paul must have had fond memories of the church in the Roman Colony of Philippi. It was the first church he founded in Europe during his second missionary journey (Acts 16).[1] And yet, as his letter unfolds, he addresses a series of disturbing issues among the Philippian believers…issues like persecution, false teachings, and conflict in the church. But it doesn't stop there. Paul also addresses the deceptive lure of Easy Street. He writes:

> *"Stick with me, friends. Keep track of those you see running this same course, headed for this same goal. There are many out there taking other paths, choosing other goals, and trying to get you to go along with them. I've warned you of them many times; sadly, I'm having to do it again. All they want is easy street. They hate Christ's Cross.* **But easy street is a dead-end street.** *Those who live there make their bellies their gods; belches are their praise; all they can think of is their appetites"* (Philippians 3:17-19, MSG, emphasis added).

Paul didn't mince words when he described Easy Street, and yet, it's still so enticing. I don't like pain. I'm guessing you don't either. There's nothing appealing about suffering, rejection, resistance, or discomfort. Indulging in luxury is far more desirable. Satisfying our appetite is much more appealing. But comfort and abundance were never meant to be our chief aim in life. They're wonderful blessings but horrible taskmasters, because the appetite for comfort is rarely satisfied.

The purpose of life is not to chase pain, but it's not to avoid pain either. Author and pastor Louie Giglio once said, "We don't choose discomfort, and that's why God usually chooses it for us."[2] God is good…so good that He calls us out of mediocrity and into a life of significance. It just so happens that a life of significance is always accompanied with some form of hardship. You can't have one without the other.

We desire a pain-free and prosperity-filled life. We seek after a problem-free path that leads us to a promise-filled future. Simply put, we spend so much of our lives pursuing Easy Street, and yet, Jesus—the greatest example of significance the world has ever known—travelled nowhere close to Easy Street. Instead, he pursued the most important eternal mission known to humanity. But it came with a high price—one pierced with nails and woven with a crown of thorns. It wasn't easy, but it was more than worth it.

Easy street is a dead-end street.

The question is, are we willing to follow His example? Are we willing to stop chasing easy and pursue a life that counts both today and for eternity?

Maybe you're pushing back, remembering Jesus' words when He said, "For my yoke is easy to bear, and the burden I give you is light" (Matthew 11:30). When Jesus spoke these words, He was contrasting what it was like to be His disciple versus that of the Pharisees. In fact, Jesus once said of the Pharisees, "They crush people with unbearable religious demands and never lift a finger to ease the burden" (Matthew 23:4). But Jesus offered a different yoke, one that was fitted with grace and love. That didn't mean life would be problem-free, nor did it void Jesus' words when He said, "If any of you wants to be my follower, you must give up your own way, take up your cross, and follow me" (Matthew 16:24). As William Barclay observed, "It is not that the burden is easy to carry; but it is laid on us in love."[3] God's grace and love gives us the power to follow Jesus and to fulfill His purpose for our lives. It doesn't erase "hard" from life.

So, what is "Easy Street"? "Easy Street" is a mindset. It's an approach to life that says, "If it's *easy* it must be good, and if it's *hard* it must be bad." Easy Street is an attitude that looks for short-cuts and makes avoiding difficulty the highest priority of life. It feels entitled to perks, influence, and opportunity without having to pay the price of discipline and risk, or endure the struggles of pain, hardship, and suffering. Easy Street is also an appetite. It's consumed with the temporal, and it gives little thought to the eternal. Every good and perfect gift comes from God (James 1:17), but Easy Street elevates the blessings of God over the God of blessings. Easy Street makes a god out of easy. It puts conformity before Christ and comfort before character. An uncontrolled appetite for easy is the Achilles' heel of Easy Street. When easy becomes the carrot, we chase it all the way to a dead-end street.

So, if we're going to stop chasing easy and pursue a life that counts, where do we start? The apostle Paul provides a roadmap in his letter to the Philippians. Yes, he clearly states that "easy street is a dead-end street," but he also paints a picture of what it looks like to pursue significance. A closer look at the four chapters in his letter reveals four keys to stop chasing easy, coupled with four unique trade-offs:

1. Mindset: Trade Pessimism for Perspective (Philippians 1)
2. Maturity: Trade Comfort for Character (Philippians 2)
3. Mission: Trade Temporal for Eternal (Philippians 3)
4. Movement: Trade Regression for Progression (Philippians 4)

These four keys—mindset, maturity, mission, and movement—are the roadmap for steering clear of the deceptive lure of Easy Street. In other words, to live a life that counts, we must cultivate the right mindset, continually grow in maturity, commit to an eternal mission, and create forward movement. So, if you're tired of chasing the empty promises of ease, comfort, and security and you're eager to do something that matters both today and for eternity, keep reading.

In the pages that follow, we'll discover Paul's insights to live a life of significance, and we'll learn how to successfully navigate the hardships that accompany it. We'll discover how to travel the road that builds impact without losing heart when obstacles, roadblocks, and resistance rear their ugly heads. Together, we'll stop chasing easy and trade it for a life that truly counts.

So, where do we begin our journey to a life that counts? It starts with mindset, as described in Philippians chapter one. Without a change in mindset, we remain trapped by the lies of Easy Street. On Easy Street, we let old thinking patterns rob meaning and purpose from our lives and bad attitudes and toxic thoughts undermine the plans God has for us. The Easy Street mindset leads us to settle for mediocrity.

However, when our mindset changes, we're able to see a way out of the neighborhood where Easy Street keeps us confined. We're empowered with an attitude that rises above riskless nonsense and boldly asks, "What if!" What does that mindset look like? Philippians one reveals that it's a...

- Thankfulness Mindset
- Growth Mindset
- Opportunity Mindset
- Big Picture Mindset
- Perseverance Mindset

These mindsets take the limits off your life. They are oriented around positivity and possibility. They enable us to trade our pessimism for a perspective that breaks through the fears and the lies that keep us tied to Easy Street. This is the first key to making your life count today... and for eternity. Let's get started.

Part 1: Mindset

Trade Pessimism for Perspective

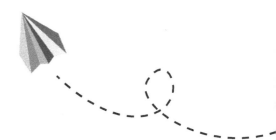

Chapter 1
Thankfulness
Embrace the Perspective of Gratitude

I t's the week of Thanksgiving as I write these words. People are heading out on vacation to visit family and friends. Office work is winding down, ovens are heating up, and recipes are being dusted off. Some are boarding flights the day before Thanksgiving (one of the busiest travel days of the year). Others are expecting family to arrive any moment. As everyone gathers around the table to give thanks, hearts will be warmed with the blessings we enjoy.

But then something strange happens.

Before the day ends, we start ramping up for an early start to *Black Friday*. The deal-buster shopping day after Thanksgiving (which often begins Thanksgiving night), Black Friday is where people hunt for the best deals on the latest gifts and gadgets. Although I usually stay home on Black Friday, I have nothing against those brave shoppers who venture into the fray. But I do find it bizarre. Each year we see the casualties of the craziness. Some people have even been trampled to death as shoppers fight to get their hands on the best bargain.

It's a modern-day version of Dr. Jekyll and Mr. Hyde. The same people who were so nice at the Thanksgiving table have transformed into beastly shopping bullies. Kind of ironic, don't you think? A holiday of *gratitude* is followed by a hectic day of *greed*. How quickly we forget.

Gratitude has also been replaced by complaints. We complain about everything from people to politics, homework to office work, and date nights to late nights. Heck, we even complain when the doctor that saved our lives doesn't check us out of the hospital quick enough. The act of complaining has become so commonplace and yet doesn't eliminate our problems, it only *extends* them.

We forget gratitude quickest when traveling down the streets of pain and suffering. The apostle Paul certainly understood this when he was under house arrest, chained to a Roman soldier, writing his letter to the church in Philippi. He was suffering, facing the threat of death, and he understood that his words to the Philippians might be his last. Paul doesn't open his letter with a gripe session, although he certainly could have. He could have griped about the length of his stay (likely imprisoned for two years). He could have complained about the uncomfortable quarters, being chained to a Roman guard, or the lack of decent food and a comfortable pillow. But he didn't. Easy Street wasn't even on his radar. Instead, Paul opened his letter with these unlikely words of gratitude:

> *May God our Father and the Lord Jesus Christ give you grace and peace. Every time I think of you,* I give thanks *to my God. Whenever I pray, I make my requests for all of you* with joy, *for you have been my partners in spreading the Good News about Christ from the time you first heard it until now. And I am certain that God, who began the good work within you, will continue his work until it is finally finished on the day when Christ Jesus returns. So it is right that I should feel as I do about all of you, for* you have a special place in my heart. *You share with me the special* favor *of God, both in my imprisonment and in defending and confirming the truth of the Good News. God knows how much* I love *you and long for you with the tender compassion of Christ Jesus. (Philippians 1:2-8, emphasis added)*

Notice the words Paul used to describe his mindset—thanks, joy, special place, favor, and love. Those sound like the words you'd hear on Easy Street, not while chained to a Roman soldier. Even though Paul's body was imprisoned, his mind was not. He faced his hardships by giving thanks for the good in the midst of the bad. That mindset served Paul well as he pursued a life that counts.

Good vs. Bad

Giving thanks is not how most of us respond to adversity, but Paul's perspective wasn't shaped by adversity; it was shaped by eternity. He was able to see beyond the physical hardship and discovered the *good*. "Good" is open for interpretation.

Most of us translate "good" to mean *easy* and "hard" to mean *bad*. If something makes life easier for us, we chalk it up as an acceptable definition of "good." But if something feels hard, we immediately throw it in the "bad" column. The problem is, we assume God takes the same approach.

He doesn't.

God's "good" is often tied to our growth, and the things that make us grow the most are rarely easy. The question is, can you, like Paul, be thankful during the hard times, recognizing these are the situations and seasons that lead to the greatest growth.

Something that helped me recognize the *good*, when things are *hard*, was a challenge I received a few years ago. I was a part of a coaching cohort with a group of pastors, and during one of our meetings our coach challenged us to keep a "Gratitude Journal" for thirty days. I thought, "No big deal, this will be easy enough." Each night, before going to bed, I would open my iPad and write down two things I was thankful for that day. When I started the journal, I focused on the big things.

"God, I'm grateful for salvation in Jesus Christ."

"God, I'm thankful for my wife Karen and our daughter Ashley and her husband Dylan."

But something unexpected happened over the course of that month. I suddenly became cognizant of the small things that I was thankful for as well. One night I wrote down how I was thankful for an unexpected dinner that Karen and I had with some friends we hadn't seen in a long time. Another time, I was thankful for rest, and another time I was thankful for Italian food. The longer I journaled, the more I began to express gratitude for the simple things in life. And because it was a *daily* practice, it forced me to find something good, even when

> *God's "good" is often tied to our growth, and the things that make us grow the most are rarely easy.*

the day was hard.

A few months later I gave this same challenge to our church: "What would happen if you took the next thirty days to write down two things you are thankful for in a gratitude journal? How would your perspective, and your life, change?"

Nearly a year later, I was having a conversation with a lady in our congregation when she suddenly said, "Oh, I can write that in my gratitude journal."

That struck me.

Gratitude journal?

She was still writing two things she was grateful for each day in her journal. The next week, I asked her to tell me more about her gratitude journey over that year.

She looked at me and said, "Each day, after I spend some time praying and reading Scripture, I open my journal and write down two things I'm grateful for that day."

"How has that impacted your life?" I asked.

"There's so much pain and difficulty in the world," she said, "that it helps me *focus* on the good."

There it was—*perspective*. Deliberately choosing to give thanks for the good, despite how dark the day might look. This simple practice had changed her life.

My wife, Karen took up the gratitude journal challenge as well, but she put a twist to it. She said, "I'm going to write down two things I'm thankful for—one is something I can see, and one is something I cannot see." I found her comment curious, so I asked her to explain. "I want to thank God for something that has already happened (something I can see with my eyes). But I also want to thank God for something that hasn't happened yet, but that I'm praying and believing God will do (something I can't see yet)."

For Karen, giving thanks had become an *act of gratitude* and an *act of faith*. I believe that God finds delight in that perspective. And if you think that gratitude is overrated, consider the science behind it.

Research has shown that people who keep a gratitude journal feel more optimistic, feel better about their lives, exercise more, and have fewer visits to the doctor.[4] And in a study of adults who reported clinically low levels of mental health (and who were seeking mental health counseling), those who also wrote one letter of gratitude per week for three weeks, experienced significantly better mental health four weeks, and again twelve weeks, after their writing exercise ended.[5]

Three Types of Thanks

Why is gratitude such an important mindset if you're going to stop chasing easy and start pursuing a life that counts? Without an attitude of gratitude, you'll complain each moment life gets hard. Your thinking will turn south, and your negative perspective will cast a shadow over the possibilities that exist beyond Easy Street. Proverbs 4:23 give us a clear warning: "Be careful what you think, because your thoughts run your life" (NCV). Without a perspective that's soaked in a spirit of thankfulness, complaining thoughts will drive your life back to Easy Street.

Without an attitude of gratitude, you'll complain each moment life gets hard. Your thinking will turn south, and your negative perspective will cast a shadow over the possibilities that exist beyond Easy Street.

So, what does thankfulness look like in our day-to-day lives? As I've reflected on the importance of gratitude, I've come to discover three forms (or maybe even three levels) of thankfulness as it relates specifically to adversity. Each one is more difficult than the previous, and honestly, from a human point of view, they seem progressively irrational.

1. END Thanks

This type of thanks usually occurs *after* something—whether good or bad—has happened. Paul practiced END Thanks when he expressed gratitude for the Philippians' partnership with the Gospel (Philippians 1:3-5). But END Thanks also shows up *after* tests and trials. For example, we might express END Thanks when we say, "Thank God I don't have to take that class again!" or "Thank God that sickness is behind me!" Simply put, "END Thanks" happens when we're out of the woods or out of the storm. It's how we give God thanks for helping us, healing us, or meeting us in our darkest hour.

2. IN Thanks

The second type of thanks occurs *during* tests and trials. Paul captured this form of thankfulness in 1 Thessalonians 5:18 when he said, "Be thankful *in* all circumstances, for this is God's will for you who belong to Christ Jesus" (emphasis added). Notice, Paul wasn't selective about his thankfulness. He gave thanks in ALL circumstances. "IN Thanks" doesn't make sense IN our pain. It requires courage and a willingness to see our circumstances from an entirely different perspective.

3. FOR Thanks

The final type of thanks feels the most irrational and unrealistic. This form of thanksgiving can take weeks, months, even years before it is realized, and there's no shame if you find yourself struggling with what I'm about to share with you. "FOR Thanks" occurs when we choose to thank God FOR the trial because of the *gifts* we received in it.

I'm not saying that God is the source of your pain. I'm not saying that God is the cause of your suffering, or that he takes joy in seeing you weep, because He isn't, and He doesn't.

There are many causes of pain, but God isn't one of them. Satan, bad decisions, people with evil intentions, and unfair circumstances outside of anyone's control are the cause of pain. But God is good, and God is the cause of every good gift (James 1:17). What we often forget is that God is so good, that He doesn't waste pain, regardless of its cause. Instead, God meets us in the middle of our pain and offers us a gift.

The apostle Paul gives us a personal example. In his second letter to the church in Corinth, Paul expressed "FOR Thanks" when he described his "thorn in the flesh" (or his handicap). He wrote:

> *Because of the extravagance of those revelations, and so I wouldn't get a big head, I was given the* gift *of a handicap to keep me in constant touch with my limitations. Satan's angel did his best to get me down; what he in fact did was push me to my knees. No danger then of walking around high and mighty! At first, I didn't think of it as a gift, and begged God to remove it. Three times I did that, and then he told me,* "My grace is enough; it's all you need. My strength comes into its own in your weakness." *Once I heard that, I was glad to let it happen. I quit focusing on the handicap and began appreciating the gift. It was a case of Christ's strength moving in on my weakness. Now I take limitations in stride, and* with good cheer, *these limitations that cut me down to size—abuse, accidents, opposition, bad breaks. I just let Christ take over! And so the weaker I get, the stronger I become.* (2 Corinthians 12:7-10, MSG, emphasis added)

Notice the phrases Paul used to describe his trial: "gift of a handicap," "I was glad to let it happen," "appreciating the gift," and "with good cheer." Paul's attitude doesn't sound like a rational response to pain and hardship. In another passage, Paul said, "I am glad when I suffer for you in my body, for I am participating in the sufferings of Christ that continue for his body, the church."[6] Paul's perspective allowed him to see his hardships correctly and give thanks FOR his tests and trials— even though they didn't come from God—because it was the very place where he received God's good gifts of *grace* and *strength*.

Pain isn't a gift from God, but within the pain He offers us a gift. It's up to us whether we'll accept His gift or not.

Pain isn't a gift from God, but within the pain He offers us a gift. It's up to us whether we'll accept His gift or not. FOR Thanks help us recognize the gift.[7] Let me give you a personal example.

Heart Failure

In 2014, I faced a hardship that introduced me to gratitude in a measure I had never known before. On March 16, my heart's mitral valve unexpectedly ruptured just nine days after my annual heart check-up. My lungs filled with fluid and I simultaneously experienced heart and pulmonary failure. I was sedated, intubated, and transported by helicopter to the heart center at Harris Hospital near downtown Fort Worth. The doctors performed open heart surgery, installed a mechanical valve, and I spent eight days in the hospital before returning home for a six-week recovery.[8]

Less than three months after my surgery, my understanding of thankfulness had completely changed. I was filled with deep gratitude to my wife, daughter, family, friends, pastors, doctors, and nurses who supported me beyond imagination. And, of course, I was thankful to the Lord for sparing my life and helping me recover.

However, gratitude also showed up in a strangely different, unexpected way during this journey. Yes, I encountered "END Thanks" when the entire ordeal was finally over. And I experienced "IN Thanks" as so many friends and family extended God's love in the most tangible ways. They prayed for me, brought meals to our family, and stepped up to help carry the load during my absence. But I'll never forget reading Paul's words in 2 Corinthians 12 and sensing the Lord say to me, "Can you thank me *for* your heart failure?"

That stopped me in my tracks.

"God, what on earth do you mean, thank you *for* my heart failure?"

It just doesn't sound right, much less feel right. I'm not looking to sign-up for heart failure or pulmonary failure again, and I certainly wouldn't want to put my family through those critical moments of uncertainty again. Besides, God didn't *cause* the heart failure. Why would I thank him *for* it?

That's when it suddenly hit me.

When thanking God for the trial, I was actually thanking Him for the *gifts* I experienced in the trial—gifts that included greater trust, bigger perspective, answers to prayer, personal and spiritual growth, and a deeper connection to my family and friends. It was all a matter of perspective. I could either focus on the *trial* or I could focus on the *gift* within the trial, it was my choice.

Again, FOR Thanks sounds irrational and illogical. In no way am I making light of your pain, abuse, brokenness, hardship, or persecution. God did not cause my heart failure, and He did not cause the horrific events that still leave you feeling violated, betrayed, forgotten, and victimized. But when pain strikes, God doesn't run for cover. He offers gifts to help us get through what we're going through. Like Paul, those gifts may be God's grace and strength in new measures and new ways. Or it might be a friend, a loved one, or a kind neighbor. It could be as simple as a co-worker's words of encouragement, or it could be as thorough as a counselor's wisdom to help you navigate the chaos. Whatever God's gifts look like, I promise He's faithful to give them to you during your most difficult seasons.

Thanks in the Thick of It

Without an attitude of gratitude, you'll complain about everything the moment it gets hard. It takes no effort whatsoever to complain about our problems or to dream about the false promises of Easy Street. That's why a mindset of gratitude is so imperative. If you're going to pursue a life that counts today—and for eternity—giving thanks in the thick of hardship equips you with the perspective that will keep you in the game.

What's your plan to embrace the mindset of thankfulness as you prepare to leave the safety of Easy Street? Why not start with a gratitude journal? It will help you put "END Thanks," "IN Thanks," and "FOR Thanks" into practice. It will turn thanksgiving into an act of gratitude *and* an act of faith. Most importantly, it will fortify your heart when you feel discouraged, and it will help you mine for hidden gifts when the path forward becomes difficult.

Chapter 2
Growth

Cultivate the Perspective of Lifelong Learning

I used to hate reading! When I was in high school, and even in college, reading was the furthest thing from my list of most desirable things to do. Could I read? Certainly. But nothing about it energized me.

All of that changed a couple of years after graduating college. I was in my first ministry position, and I was sinking. Things were not going as planned. All the neatly packaged answers I learned in Bible college weren't answering the questions asked of me. I felt prepared for irrelevance. As American social writer Eric Hoffer once observed, "In times of change, learners inherit the earth, while the learned find themselves beautifully equipped to deal with a world that no longer exists."[9] Needless to say, I was in over my head.

In the years that followed, slowly but intentionally, I developed a healthy habit of reading. I picked up John Maxwell's early book, *Developing the Leader Within You*, and I devoured every word. When I was finished, I remember thinking, "This is the best leadership book I've ever read." Then it dawned on me: "This is the *only* leadership book I've ever read." But my journey had begun. More important than a habit of reading, I was developing a habit of growing.[10]

A few years later I attended a lunch gathering with 300 leaders where John Maxwell was featuring his newly released book, *The 21 Irrefutable Laws of Leadership*. During his speech, Dr. Maxwell talked about The Law of Process which says that "Leadership develops daily, not in a day."

At the end of his teaching, he gave us a challenge that grabbed my attention more than any other: create a plan for personal growth. By this time, I had developed a habit of reading, but I didn't have a focused, personalized growth plan that was guiding my daily development. Growth was happening, but at times it felt haphazard.

> *A dream is a beautiful picture of the future, but between you and your dream is a gap. The only way to close that gap is to grow into the kind of person that can actually reach your dream.*

My first attempt at a growth plan was to purchase an audio cassette curriculum (this was back in the 90's) based on the 21 Laws. I decided to come into the office an hour early each day, listen to a leadership tape, capture my thoughts in a workbook, and then apply what I was learning to my life and leadership. My growth plan wasn't rocket science, but it was helping me raise my leadership lid.

Raise Your Lid

Somewhere along the way, you're going to hit a lid in your life. Your lid is the ceiling that limits the impact and the outcomes of your life. You might experience a lid in your career, finances, relationships, or health. At that moment, you have a choice to make: do I let the lid confine me to Easy Street, or do I grow past it? Those are really your only two options. The choice to grow past your limits is what brings your dreams into your reach.

A dream is a beautiful picture of the future, but between you and your dream is a gap. The only way to close that gap is to grow into the kind of person that can actually reach your dream. Truthfully, somebody in the world is probably already living your dream. Why? Because they closed their growth gap. They grew from where they were to where they needed to be (and from who they were into who they needed to become). You have to do the same, or your dream will remain just that—a dream. Nothing more. Growth is the price tag you pay to turn the dream into reality.

Growth is rarely found on Easy Street. As C.S. Lewis once said, "God allows us to experience the low points of life in order to teach us lessons we could not learn in any other way."[11] Besides, Easy Street will tell you that you don't *need* to grow. Why? Because Easy Street isn't interested in paying the price tag of growth. It only wants to reap the rewards. And yet you can't have one without the other.

If you're going to stop chasing easy and pursue a life that counts, you'll need to develop a mindset (and a habit) of disciplined growth. Growth requires discipline, and discipline is its own form of difficulty. As the old saying goes, "You can live with the pain of discipline or the pain of regret." Your perspective toward growth will determine which one you choose.

Four Growth Guides

The apostle Paul understood the importance of a growth mindset when he wrote these words: "I pray that your love will overflow more and more, and that you will *keep on growing* in knowledge and understanding. For I want you to understand what really matters, so that you may live pure and blameless lives until the day of Christ's return. May you always be filled with the fruit of your salvation—the righteous character produced in your life by Jesus Christ—for this will bring much glory and praise to God" (Philippians 1:9-11, emphasis added). These three verses contain four guides for growth. Each one will help you put the brakes on a passive life and help you accelerate into the future with a robust growth mindset.

1. Growth is Continual

Paul challenged his readers to "keep on growing in knowledge and understanding." He wasn't suggesting a one-time conference or a single book to meet an annual growth quota. "Keep on growing" implies a growth habit and a commitment to lifelong learning. Growth is a process, not an event. While events can inspire change, processes create change and habits sustain change. You can attend an event to inspire your growth, but after the event is over, you still need to engage in a continual process of personal growth where you can develop the habits that sustain your growth and change.

2. Growth is Purposeful

Paul continues, "For I want you to understand what really matters…" In other words, Paul wanted the growth his readers experienced to be extremely purposeful. Why? So they would "live pure and blameless lives until the day of Christ's return." They had to grow in a purposeful area (character) and for a continual length of time (until Christ returns).

3. Growth is Fruitful

Paul continues, "May you always be filled with the fruit of your salvation—the righteous character produced in your life by Jesus Christ." That's what growth does—it produces fruit. In this case, Paul called that fruit "righteous character." In case you haven't noticed, character grows in the hard seasons of life much more than the easy seasons. Easy Street desires fruit, but it doesn't have the capacity to produce it. That's why having a growth perspective is essential in the hardships of life. The right perspective makes fruit-bearing possible.

> **Character grows in the hard seasons of life much more than the easy seasons.**

4. Growth is Reproducible

Finally, Paul wasn't concerned solely about his own spiritual growth. He took a deliberate interest in the growth of others. His passion for the church in Philippi to thrive is seen in his prayers, instruction, and his challenge to these believers. Paul didn't just model growth; he inspired it in others.

When you encounter hardships, Satan has one goal—to bring you down. He wants to eliminate you, or at the very least neutralize your effectiveness. God, on the other hand, has another goal—to enlarge you. King David said, "God, you are my righteousness, my champion defender. Answer me when I cry for help! Whenever I was in distress, *you enlarged me*" (Psalm 4:1a, TPT, emphasis added). You get to choose your response to distress: it can crush you or it can enlarge you. Both options come with pain, but only one comes with the promise of growth.

Author and consultant Sam Chand observed, "You will grow only to the threshold of your pain."[12] Pain can be either a cap or a catalyst to your growth, depending on your perspective. In other words, if you have the wrong perspective toward pain, it will limit your growth, but if you have the right perspective toward pain, it will be a launching pad for your growth. King Solomon said, "Sorrow is better than laughter, for sadness has a refining influence on us" (Ecclesiastes 7:3). Most of us let sadness have a negative influence on us, but when we choose a growth mindset, it can refine and enlarge us.

How to Grow

Because growth is a continual and purposeful process that helps you make your life count, you need a system to help you grow for a lifetime. Coupled with a growth perspective, you need a growth plan. I told you earlier about my first growth plan. Since then, each year I create what I call a "Growth TRAC." Having a Growth TRAC is how you create, implement, and then monitor your

---

Sam Chand observed, *"You will grow only to the threshold of your pain."*

---

own plan for personal growth.[13] A Growth TRAC includes four steps (each accompanied by a growth question):

Target: What are My Growth Goals?

A Growth TRAC begins by identifying the *Target* you hope to reach. In other words, in what area of your life do you want to grow? Jesus' growth was focused on four areas: spiritual, mental, relational, and physical. Luke 2:52 says, "And Jesus grew in wisdom and stature, and in favor with God and man" (NIV). Choosing specific growth goals is usually the easiest part of the process because most people have an intuitive sense of the areas of life they want to improve, grow, or expand. Let those areas become your growth Targets.

Roadmap: How Do I Plan to Grow?

Once you identify the areas you want to grow, you need to develop a *Roadmap* to get there. When you drive to a new destination, you always begin with the target (your ending point). When you enter that target into your favorite mapping app, it gives you a roadmap to follow. That roadmap will include a variety of roads, turns, and detailed instructions. The same is true with a Growth TRAC. Your Roadmap consists of a series of growth steps to help you arrive at your desired destination. Those growth steps are typically things like training, resources, coaching, and experiences. For example, if you set a Target to get out of debt in the next 18 months, you might attend a financial seminar (training), read a book on how to eliminate debt (resource), meet with a financial advisor (coaching), and create a new budget (experience). Each step forms a Roadmap to help you reach your Target of being debt free.

Accountability: Who Will Hold Me Accountable for My Growth?

This step is the easiest to avoid, but avoiding steps to growth will keep you cruising towards the dead end of Easy Street. To grow to your full potential, you need somebody to hold your feet to the fire and help you build *Accountability*. You're still responsible for your own growth (after all, you can't delegate growth), but most of us aren't good enough to grow for a lifetime without the support and encouragement of friends and mentors. If you really want this step to work, give your accountability partner the questions you want them to ask you each time you meet. These questions will elevate the intentionality of your growth. Using the financial illustration above, you might have a friend ask you questions like: "How much debt did you eliminate this month?"; "What advice did your financial advisor give you?"; "How much of your book did you read, and what was your greatest take-away?"; or "What changes have you made to your budget to help you reach your goal?"

Check-Up: When and How Will I Evaluate My Growth Progress?

The final part of the Growth TRAC, *Check-Up*, is designed to help you measure your progress in a time-sensitive manner. How often will you do a check-up to measure your progress toward your Target? What deadlines will you attach to the various steps in your Roadmap? The key is to do a check-up frequently enough to keep your goal in focus, and to make any mid-course corrections that could improve your growth outcomes.

If you're going to pursue a life that counts both today and for eternity, you need to develop a growth mindset. A lifelong learning attitude will thrust you out of your comfort zone on Easy Street and into the zone where growth is realized and maximized. Why not get started today? Create, implement, and monitor your own Growth TRAC, and then watch the gap close between you and your dreams.

Chapter 3
Opportunity
Choose the Perspective of Possibility

S amuel Truett Cathy is remembered as the successful entrepreneur
and founder of Chick-fil-A. Cathy died in 2014, but his quick-ser-
vice restaurants continue to thrive today. In fact, each Chick-fil-A
makes more money per store than McDonalds, Starbucks, and Subway
combined.[14]

My wife met Truett Cathy years ago when she worked for an airline
in Lexington, Kentucky. She acknowledged who Mr. Cathy was as he
was checking in for a flight. His demeanor and response were kind and
considerate as he pulled out a copy of his book, *Eat Mor Chikin: Inspire
More People*, signed it, and then gave it to Karen.

While the success of Chick-fil-A is obvious, what you may not know
about is the struggle that Truett Cathy experienced along the way. He
grew up in the Great Depression and regularly helped his mom in the
kitchen while she ran a boarding house. Truett's father lost his farm in
the early 20s and eventually sold insurance, but he never fully recovered
from this loss.[15] In 1935, they moved into the country's first federally
subsidized housing project—Techwood Homes.

Truett developed an entrepreneurial spirit early in his life. When he
was only eight years old, he would buy a six pack of Coca Colas for
twenty-five cents and sell them door-to-door for a nickel each, making
five cents profit per six-pack. Eventually his sales grew to the point that
he was buying 24 cokes for eighty cents from the Coca-Cola truck,
doubling his profit per case. With his profits he bought a bicycle, and at

the age of twelve, Truett started his own paper route. He did his best to treat every customer with the greatest respect. "I delivered each paper as if I were delivering it to the front door of the governor's mansion" Truett said.[16] With his knack for business and entrepreneurship, he came to understand the importance of taking care of the customer.

On May 23, 1946, after serving in the Army during World War II, Truett and his brother Ben opened a 24-hour restaurant, the Dwarf Grill, in Hapeville, Georgia (later renamed the Dwarf House). Sales on that opening day were $58.20. Alternating 12-hour shifts, Truett's focus from his childhood years remained his focus as an adult—serving people. He even sent food to customers during their time of need—whether sick in the hospital or grieving the loss of a family member. It was Truett's belief that every customer should be treated like the President of the United States.[17]

Truett's hard work paid off. In 1967, he opened the first Chick-fil-A (the "A" is capitalized on purpose to mean "grade A top quality") in a 384 square foot space in Greenbriar Mall in Atlanta, Georgia. Today, Chick-fil-A has over 2,500 restaurants, and has received multiple awards for their customer service and workplace environment.[18]

Truett Cathy's success is quite impressive, and from the outside, it would be easy to think he had a relatively easy path forward. But Truett didn't travel down Easy Street to arrive at so much success. Quite the opposite. Hardship found a friend in Truett, all the way back to his childhood

When Truett was selling Coca-Colas door-to-door, he had a speech impediment so bad that he couldn't even pronounce his own name.[19] In 1949, Truett's brothers, Ben and Horace (both licensed pilots), tragically died in a plane crash as they flew to Chattanooga, Tennessee. Truett later wrote, "The loss hit me particularly hard on Monday morning. When I saw where Ben made out the report sheet on Saturday morning in good health, I realized again that he would never be back, and my tears flowed."[20]

That wasn't the end of Truett's troubles. In 1951, he opened a second location of the Dwarf Grill, but on February 24, 1960, he received a phone call at 1:30 in the morning, "Mr. Cathy, your restaurant in Forest Park is on fire." Shortly after arriving on the scene, he found a host of firemen working vigorously to put out the fire. Suddenly, the roof collapsed, and everything was destroyed. The worst part? Truett only had $25,000 worth of insurance, not near enough to cover his loss.[21]

If things weren't bad enough, two days later Truett mentioned to his wife Jeannette that he had passed some blood. After she insisted he see a doctor, Truett scheduled an appointment only to discover he had polyps in his colon and would need to have surgery. Following a painful recovery, the polyps returned six months later and a second surgery was scheduled to remove twelve inches of Truett's colon.[22]

What enabled Truett Cathy to successfully navigate his setbacks? The right perspective. He exchanged pessimism for possibility. He looked for the right opportunities in the uncomfortable and the unexpected.

While we admire his success, the hardships made Truett Cathy. He later said, "The history of Chick-fil-A, in fact, is a series of unexpected opportunities. When we responded to them, we often found ourselves richly blessed. The Chick-fil-A Chicken Sandwich itself was born in the wake of an unexpected opportunity. When one of my first two restaurants burned to the ground, I found myself with time on my hands and the availability to develop a new recipe."[23] Cathy could have wallowed in defeat—most people would if they so many hours of hard work burn up in flames. Instead, Truett discovered a billion-dollar idea in the ashes.

What enabled Truett Cathy to successfully navigate his setbacks? The right perspective. He exchanged pessimism for possibility. He looked for the right opportunities in the uncomfortable and the unexpected.

That opportunistic mindset followed Truett into his philanthropic activities. "A chance encounter with a teenage boy who had lost his parents led to opportunities that have resulted in the establishment of the Chick-fil-A WinShape Centre Foundation, which supports foster homes, summer camps, and college scholarships, touching the lives of thousands of children and young adults—and literally saving some of them."[24] Truett once said, "We change the world, and ourselves, by our response to unexpected opportunities."

Seeing Opportunity Beyond Easy Street

I don't know where Truett Cathy acquired his optimistic outlook, but it's the kind of perspective that changes your life, especially when you want to make life count. The apostle Paul modeled this same perspective when he wrote, "I want to report to you, friends, that my imprisonment here has had the opposite of its intended effect. Instead of being squelched, the Message has actually prospered. All the soldiers here, and everyone else, too, found out that I'm in jail because of this Messiah. That piqued their curiosity, and now they've learned all about him. Not only that, but most of the followers of Jesus here have become far more sure of themselves in the faith than ever, speaking out fearlessly about God, about the Messiah" (Philippians 1:12-14, MSG).

Paul found opportunity beyond Easy Street. He didn't sulk in his circumstances or lose sight of his mission amidst the difficulty and discomfort. Instead, he shared the Gospel with the very soldiers he was chained to. As a result, the Gospel "prospered." The word *prospered* refers to the idea of moving forward despite the obstacles and opposition that stand in the way. In other words, the Gospel advanced through this adversity.

> *Your perspective, how you see is always more important than what you see; you can't seize what you don't see correctly.*

Not only did the Gospel prosper in Paul's circumstances, but other followers of Jesus were emboldened to speak fearlessly about the Messiah. It all started with Paul's perspective. He chose to see possibility in his problems, and as a result unleashed a wave of possibility both inside and outside of his prison.

Seeing Possibility in Your Problems

Author Hal Urban once wrote, "Once we accept the fact that life is hard, we begin to grow. We begin to understand that every problem is also an opportunity. It is then that we dig down and discover what we're made of. We begin to accept the challenges of life. Instead of letting our hardships defeat us, we welcome them as a test of character. We use them as a means of rising to the occasion."[25]

When you make the choice to stop chasing easy and start pursuing God-given opportunities, you rise to the occasion. You accept the fact that life is hard, and you grow in the face of the problems that you see. But your perspective, *how* you see is always more important than *what* you see; you can't seize what you don't see correctly. This deliberate mindset shift happens by taking the following four steps.

1. Embrace the Problem

Problems are difficult, discouraging, and often downright painful. That's why we like to ignore them. In fact, our tendency is to only address problems in two situations—when they're easy to solve or when they've become a crisis too big to ignore. It's in the messy middle that we pretend problems don't exist. But when you ignore your problems, you also ignore the opportunities buried within them. Stop pretending the problem doesn't exist. Embrace it and eliminate the paralysis it's causing in your life.

2. Examine the Problem

To discover possibilities in your problems, you have to adequately diagnose the problem. Embracing it forces you to deal with the problem, but examining it gets to the root cause. If you don't understand what caused the problem, you're likely to repeat it. So, examine the problem by asking "Why?" Not just once. Five times.

Sakichi Toyoda, founder of Toyota, developed a diagnostic approach which became popular in the 1970s, and is still used by Toyota today. The strategy is simple—define a problem and then ask "Why?" five times until you get to the root cause of the issue.[26] For example, if your problem is that you're deep in debt, then ask: 1) Why? *Because I've maxed out my credit cards.* 2) Why? *Because when I see something I like, I buy it.* 3) Why? *Because I feel a need to have it.* 4) Why? *Because I feel a need to impress my friends.* 5) Why? *Because I've anchored my value to the approval of my friends.* Bingo! You've just drilled down to the core issue. Without this process, you could have easily said, "I'm in debt because I don't make enough money," when in reality, the size of your paycheck has nothing to do with it.

3. Explore the Possibilities

Once you've uncovered the root cause, you can start exploring the possible solution (or opportunity) hidden within your problem. Using the "deep debt" illustration above, the hidden opportunity isn't to address your income but rather your identity. In other words, rather than attaching your value to the opinions of others, make an exchange—attach your value to what God says about you in His Word.

4. Engage the Possibility

It's not enough to discover the possibility; you must act on it.

Opportunity comes to life when we act on our new discovery. Paul didn't just explore the possibility of sharing the Gospel when curiosity awoke in the minds of the prison guards; he courageously engaged the opportunity.

I don't know what problem you're facing today, or perhaps I should say *problems* (most of us have a few to choose from). Hidden somewhere in that problem is an opportunity. That's what Truett Cathy discovered after his restaurant burned to the ground. He embraced and examined the problem, and then he explored and engaged the possibilities within it. That possibility was a chicken sandwich that gave birth to Chick-fil-A. It all started with a shift in perspective. The perspective of possibility is essential if you're going to stop chasing easy and pursue a life that counts. It's what allows you to see past the empty pursuits of easy street and into a future filled with God-inspired dreams.

Chapter 4
Big Picture
Nurture a "See and Serve" Perspective

Several years ago, Karen and I visited The Metropolitan Museum of Art in New York City. "The Met" houses a wide range of art—everything from modern art to European sculptures, from the Arts of Africa to Egyptian Art.

During this particular visit, the Museum featured the works of the famous French painter Eugene Delacroix. For more than four decades, Delacroix produced rich paintings that included literature, history, religion, and more. Two things that made Eugene Delacroix famous were his optical effects and intense brushstrokes.[27] Each stroke brought the visions in his mind's eye to life. But, as with any painting, to truly enjoy its beauty, you can't focus on the individual brushstrokes. The beauty is experienced when you see the whole picture.

Unfortunately, we don't always see life that way. We have a tendency to let the individual brushstrokes of our circumstances consume us. That's especially true when we consider that the painting of our lives is still a work in progress. It requires perspective to step back—while the painting is in progress—and see the big picture.

Therein lies the tension.

The big picture is what matters most, but you can't have the big picture without the individual brushstrokes. And yet, if an artist only focused on each brushstroke, there would be no rhyme or reason to their artwork. Yes, they paint one stroke at a time, but they do so with the big picture in mind.

This is how God works in our lives. Some strokes are happy and fun, while others are difficult. Some strokes are bold and bright, while others seem to go unnoticed. God doesn't waste a single stroke. He uses every paint color imaginable—the beautiful colors born out of His goodness, and the bland colors we hand to him through our bad decisions and painful problems. He blends them together to form a masterpiece that only makes sense when you view it with a wide-angle lens.

> **God doesn't waste a single stroke. He uses every paint color imaginable— the beautiful colors born out of His goodness, and the bland colors we hand to him through our bad decisions and painful problems.**

Seeing the big picture is a critical choice, to stop chasing easy. Granted, sometimes it's difficult to make sense of the big picture, especially when a few brushstrokes seem completely out of place. Nonetheless, it's still our decision to take a few steps back and ask God to help us see life from His perspective. When we do, we position ourselves to cooperate with God's handiwork in our lives. Rather than focusing on our limited view, we welcome the wide-angle wisdom of the Master Painter.

Seeing the Big Picture

The apostle Paul had to make a very deliberate choice to see the big picture when he was in prison. During his confinement, others were preaching the Gospel, but their motives for doing so were self-serving at best. With the brushstrokes of that reality covering the walls of his prison cell, Paul wrote these words:

> *"It's true that some are preaching out of jealousy and rivalry. But others preach about Christ with pure motives. They preach because they love me, for they know I have been appointed to defend the Good News. Those others do not have pure motives as they preach about Christ. They preach with selfish ambition, not sincerely, intending to make my chains more painful to me"* *(Philippians 1:15-17).*

Paul could have stopped there, or he could have gone off on a rant, criticizing and complaining about every brushstroke of insincerity and selfish ambition. Instead, Paul focused on the big picture—*Christ is preached*—when he wrote: "But that doesn't matter. Whether their motives are false or genuine, the message about Christ is being preached either way, so I rejoice. And I will continue to rejoice." (Philippians 1:18).

Paul had the perspective to keep his eye on the big picture and let God deal with the hearts of those who preached with impure motives. Rather than criticizing everything wrong in the church, Paul actually "rejoiced" that the Gospel was being preached. He didn't respond to jealousy with more jealousy, or to insincerity with insecurity. He rejoiced and then said, "And I will *continue* to rejoice."

How freeing that must have been for Paul. While chained to a guard, he refuses to be emotionally and mentally chained by other preachers' impure motives. Most of us in that situation would be constrained by the very thing we cannot control. We would focus on brushstrokes of jealousy, and then start slinging our own accusatory paint onto a canvas of condemnation. Instead, a big-picture perspective *sees* God's plan right so that it can *serve* right.

Serving the Big Picture

Paul didn't know what the outcome of his situation would be: released from prison or put to death. The future was uncertain. But one thing was clear to Paul—he was in a win-win situation. Life or death, Paul would triumph. He continued the expression of his big-picture outlook with these words:

> *For I know that as you pray for me and the Spirit of Jesus Christ helps me, this will lead to my deliverance. For I fully expect and hope that I will never be ashamed, but that I will continue to be bold for Christ, as I have been in the past. And I trust that my life will bring honor to Christ, whether I live or die. For to me, living means living for Christ, and dying is even better. But if I live, I can do more fruitful work for Christ. So I really don't know which is better. I'm torn between two desires: I long to go and be with Christ, which would be far better for me. But for your sakes, it is better that I continue to live. Knowing this, I am convinced that I will remain alive so*

I can continue to help all of you grow and experience the joy of your faith. And when I come to you again, you will have even more reason to take pride in Christ Jesus because of what he is doing through me. (Philippians 1:19-26)

Paul was torn between two desires—to live would mean "fruitful work for Christ," and to die would mean eternity with Christ. In other words, life, or more life. It was a win-win proposition. In the midst of the tug-of-war, Paul determined, "for your sakes, it is better that I continue to live." Why? So that he could continue to preach the Gospel. Simply put, Paul kept his eye on the big picture so that he could ultimately *serve* the purpose God had called him to.

> **To nurture a big picture perspective, you have to intentionally see it and then deliberately serve it.**

Here's the point—Paul had the ability to do both: *see* and *serve* the big picture. When wrong motives could have distracted him, he didn't lose sight of the fact that the Gospel was still being preached. And when death would have looked attractive (especially considering his circumstances), Paul was convinced that his call to serve God's mission wasn't over. He was determined to make his life count for eternity. He could *see* the big picture with certainty and was committed to *serve* the big picture with eagerness.

The same should be true for us.

To nurture a big picture perspective, you have to intentionally *see it* and then deliberately *serve it*. But it always starts with *seeing*. Unless you first step back and see the big picture, you'll never know how to serve it.

Defeating Big-Picture Inhibitors

Two false beliefs usually inhibit a big-picture mindset: *limitless problems* and *limited possibilities*. First, we falsely believe that our problems are limitless, and as a result, they consume our view. We let the pain in our painting define the entire canvas. Second, we falsely believe the possibilities that exist beyond our view are limited. We interpret the entire painting with a scarcity mentality, only embracing what we can see up close. Both beliefs are false, and both beliefs will disrupt any attempts to see and serve the big picture. So, how do you deal with these two misguided inhibitors to big-picture perspective?

When it comes to *problems*, you have to see them for what they are—momentary setbacks that mark a very small part of your life. When Karen worked in an alternative school with students who had been suspended from the main campus, she often had to remind them that this unfortunate event didn't define their entire lives. She would go to the board, draw a long line, and then put a small mark on the line. Then she'd say, "This long line represents your life, and this tiny mark represents your time in suspension." Then she'd look at the students and say, "Be careful not to let the small mark define the entire line of your life." The students needed that illustration to help them see the big picture.

When a drop of paint from the paint can of despair finds its way onto the canvas of your life, it's often all you'll see. It consumes you. You start to think that the entire picture is ruined, and you suddenly give the blemish naming rights on your life. Resist that urge. Don't overreact. Instead, rise above the problem and see the big picture. The problem is just a brushstroke, not the entire painting.

When it comes to *possibilities*, you have to dream beyond your limited view of Easy Street. On Easy Street, a picture-perfect image of effortless ease will rest on the end of your nose. If this picture is all you see, the possibilities of your life will be limited to a fraction of your God-given potential.

Don't settle for that tiny picture. Make your life count today—and for eternity—by opening your eyes to the larger canvas beyond your nearsighted view. Let the brushstrokes of significance invade the blank space that exists beyond your periphery. Dip your brush in the paint of purpose and start filling the empty space with a bold vision. It starts by *seeing* bigger so you can *serve* bigger. If you don't see bigger, you'll never extend the borders of your life beyond the self-serving limits of Easy Street. Stop looking at your street. Get outside of the neighborhood of mediocrity and look at the possibilities that exist in your world. I'll show you how to do this later, but for now, embrace a big-picture mindset that puts problems

> *If you don't see bigger, you'll never extend the borders of your life beyond the self-serving limits of Easy Street.*

in perspective and embraces a "see and serve" approach to future possibilities.

Seeing So I Could Serve

Several years ago, we launched a major vision campaign at 7 City Church (the church I pastor near downtown Fort Worth). Vision campaigns are bold efforts to do something new (like building a new facility or launching a new ministry), and they're usually accompanied by equally bold financial investments. The challenge for us was that we were only twenty-nine weeks old as a church. Launching a bold vision that requires significant financial resources when you're less than eight months old feels risky. I still remember another pastor telling me, "Don't you think it's a bit too soon to launch a campaign?" Another man told me, "I've never seen campaigns like this go well."

When you hear comments like that, it's easy to feel caught in the space between vision and reality, between faith and fear, between a limited picture and a big picture. But I understood that if we didn't take this step, it would unnecessarily delay what needed to happen to paint the blank canvas beyond our immediate reach. We wouldn't be able to expand our team and do the groundwork for future expansion.

It was very easy in that moment to get distracted by the brushstrokes of fear. It certainly would have been a "reasonable" and "acceptable"—even "prudent"—thing to avoid such a risky step this early in our church planting journey. But deep down I knew what God was calling us to do.

Was it risky? Certainly! Was it uncomfortable? Yes! But was it worth it? Absolutely! We raised the funds needed to advance our vision, grow our team, and prepare for the future.

What about you? What is keeping you from *seeing* and *serving* the big picture? What problems, distractions, or naysayers are highlighting the difficult brushstrokes in your life and robbing your view of the wide-open space yet to be painted? Make a decision to shift your perspective today. Adopt a big-picture mindset that puts problems in their proper perspective and uncovers possibilities beyond Easy Street. This mindset will prepare you and propel you into a life that counts. When you *see it*, then you'll be able to confidently *serve it*.

Chapter 5
Perseverance
Develop the Perspective of Grit

Pursuing a life that counts is hard work. You'll want to throw in the towel more than once, and sometimes you'll wonder if the hard work is even worth it. Other times you'll feel like you're trying to move Mount Everest with a garden shovel. "I quit" sounds like a much easier path, and most people wouldn't blame you.

If you choose this path and follow Easy Street for a few years, eventually the bullhorn of regret will wake you up every morning with the shouts of "shoulda, coulda, woulda." It will remind you of everything you had hoped to become, and then it will shame you with the price tag you were unwilling to pay. The rearview mirror will taunt you as the window in front of you faces a dead-end street.

Here's the reality. Everybody pays a price. The question is, will you pay it now or later? If you pay it at the end of life, your price comes with regret, yet if you pay it now your price comes with grit. Simply put, if you want your life to count, it will require a mindset of perseverance.

In the early 1970's, sociologist Dr. Edward Banfield from Harvard University published his research on what allowed people to become financially independent. Initially, he suspected their good fortune would be credited to their education, race, family background, intelligence, or social connections. What he learned surprised him. Dr. Banfield discovered that "long time perspective" was the biggest predictor of financial success. Simply put, their decisions today were made with tomorrow in mind.[28]

What about you? Do you have "long time perspective"? Do you make decisions today with tomorrow in mind, or is your perspective limited to the here and now? Are you focused solely on today, or can you see the consequences of your decisions beyond the comfort of the moment? If you really want to create long-term change and pursue a life that counts, you need to recognize the compounding effect of a *perseverance perspective*. Robert Morrison is a perfect example.

The Compounding Effect of Perseverance

Robert Morrison was a missionary from England, called to serve the people of China. He supported himself through his work with the East India Company, but his greatest passion was his literary work.

> *Do you have "long time perspective"? Do you make decisions today with tomorrow in mind, or is your perspective limited to the here and now?*

In 1813, Morrison completed the translation of a New Testament into Chinese, and in 1819, with his colleague William Milne, they completed the translation of the entire Bible. One of his greatest accomplishments was a three-volume Chinese-English Dictionary.[29]

Morrison encountered plenty of hardship during his lifetime—hostility toward his work, the death of a child, and the death of his wife Mary and his close colleague William Milne—just to name a few. But he *never* quit.

> *"The monumental literary achievements, not to mention other aspects of his ministry, which were all wrought in an atmosphere of constant pressure from Chinese government and the EIC [East India Company], flowed from a man whose character is described as marked by 'untiring perseverance,' 'the most ardent zeal - [and] indefatigable diligence.' Beset by headaches, fatigue, and multiple physical ailments; always conscious that his Chinese helpers, his precious books and printing-blocks, and his own person could be at any time threatened by Chinese officials; restrained both by law and by the labor required by his job with the EIC; far from home and friends; working alone most of the time; longing for his family—Morrison started from*

almost nothing and built an edifice of scholarship surpassed by few." [30]

Although he saw very few converts in China, Robert Morrison's *"untiring perseverance"* set the stage for the extraordinary impact of missionaries that followed him, such as Hudson Taylor. Author Craig Groeschel once said, "The way you grow is through, not out." [31] That was Morrison's mindset. He didn't look for a way out of the hardship; instead, his perseverance enabled him to grow through it.

Morrison earned compounding interest on the bank account of perseverance. It not only produced fruit in his own life, but it left an inheritance for future generations. That kind of perseverance requires long-term perspective. Without it, you'll never make it beyond your driveway on Easy Street. Without it, you'll never build your greatest legacy.

Paul on Long-Term Perspective

Perhaps Morrison learned his perseverance perspective from the apostle Paul. Paul was determined to produce fruitful ministry—even when it was hard—and his "no quit" attitude is evident in Philippians 1:27-30. A closer look reveals three distinct qualities of Paul's persevering mindset.

First, perseverance is unconditional: Paul said, "Meanwhile, live in such a way that you are a credit to the Message of Christ. Let nothing in your conduct hang on whether I come or not. Your conduct must be the same whether I show up to see things for myself or hear of it from a distance" (Philippians 1:27a, MSG). In other words, don't tie your conduct to the conditions around you. Live your life true to the message of Jesus, regardless of who is (or isn't) looking. This is the kind of character built by true perseverance. It's not based on convenient conditions. It doesn't endure one day and relax the next, distracted by laziness and lethargy. There's an intrinsic drive to persevere unconditionally until God's plan for our lives is complete.

Second, perseverance is unflinching: Paul continued, "Stand united, singular in vision, contending for people's trust in the Message, the good news, not flinching or dodging in the slightest before the opposition. Your courage and unity will show them what they're up against: defeat for them, victory for you—and both because of God" (Philippians 1:27b-28, MSG). Look at the words Paul uses—"stand," "singular," "contending," "not flinching or dodging." People who make the greatest impact don't flinch in the face of opposition. They stick to their beliefs—both when it's easy and when it's hard, when they experience a reprieve, or when the cost is high. Everything comes in seasons, but the resolute have an unflinching perseverance to do what counts no matter what the day may bring.

Third, perseverance is undeterred: Paul concludes his remarks with these words: "There's far more to this life than trusting in Christ. There's also suffering for him. And the suffering is as much a gift as the trusting. You're involved in the same kind of struggle you saw me go through, on which you are now getting an updated report in this letter" (Philippians 1:29-30, MSG). Imagine that! Suffering should not deter our commitment to persevere. That's not a very common message in our culture today, but Paul was clear—don't quit. Embrace a perseverance that is undeterred by opposition, suffering, and unpredictable twists and turns.

> *Everything comes in seasons, but the resolute have an unflinching perseverance to do what counts no matter what the day may bring.*

The very word, "perseverance," implies these three qualities. If your perseverance isn't unconditional, unflinching, and undeterred, is it really perseverance? Consider the opposite: when something is conditional, flinches easily, or is quickly deterred, does the word "perseverance" even cross your mind? Probably not. We'd be more likely to think of words like *uncommitted* or *unfocused*. While that might be the easy path, it's certainly not the best path. The best path is always commitment—not just in word, but in action. As author Shola Richards said, "Commitment is doing what you said you would do long after the mood you said it in has left you."[32]

Pace and Purpose

Angela Lee Duckworth, author and psychologist from the University of Pennsylvania, has done extensive research on the subject of grit. She observed: "Grit is passion and perseverance for very long-term goals. Grit is having stamina. Grit is sticking with your future, day in day out, not just for the week, not just for the month, but for years, and working really hard to make that future a reality. Grit is living life like it's a marathon, not a sprint."[33]

In a sprint, the goal is always in sight, but in a marathon, you must trust what you cannot yet see. That's why so many marathoners call it quits around the 21-mile mark. They "hit the wall," and the finish line is nowhere in sight. At this point, your body has burned through its energy stores, and now it begins to metabolize your fat. Everything inside of you screams, "It's time to quit" as your body is tested to its limits. The problem is, your mind is tested too.[34] The longer you run, the more your body starts directing oxygen and nutrients to your muscles. Simply put, the mind gets weaker the longer you run, and it's the weakest when you "hit the wall."[35]

> **Pace** *is all about what you do before you hit the wall. You have to focus on your Should Do Pace, not your Could Do Pace.*

So, what do you do when everything inside of you wants to throw in the towel? You can consume some power food to boost your blood sugar, or you can use some helpful techniques to improve your running form. But if you're going to persevere to the finish line, you also need to make a mental shift to *Pace and Purpose.*

Pace is all about what you do *before* you hit the wall. You have to focus on your Should Do Pace, not your Could Do Pace. Your Could Do Pace is how fast you can ultimately run (it's running full throttle like there's no tomorrow). But just because you *can* doesn't mean you *should.* In the early part of the race, you have to pace yourself, protecting your reserves for later in the race. That's your Should Do Pace—a slightly slower pace in the first five miles to ensure you have appropriate reserves in the last five miles.

Purpose is the second key to remember when you hit the wall. Purpose is the "why" behind the "what." It's the reason you signed up for the marathon in the first place. Focusing on your purpose ignites your intrinsic motivation and gives you the extra push to keep putting one foot in front of the other. When you feel completely depleted, purpose is often all you have left to get you across the finish line.

By practicing *Pace and Purpose*, you'll be prepared when you hit the unanticipated "21-mile mark." It inevitably shows up anytime you're doing something worthwhile. *Pace* will give you the energy to keep going, and *Purpose* will give you the reason to keep going (we'll dive deeper into purpose in part three).

When you feel completely depleted, purpose is often all you have left to get you across the finish line.

Leaving Easy Street requires grit. Without this perspective, you'll return home to safety and security as soon as things get tough. You must push through what you're going through so you can get to what you're going to. That takes a persevering mindset.

The "Stop Chasing Easy" Mindset

Over the last five chapters, I've challenged you to trade pessimism for perspective. I've equipped you with the mindsets to stop chasing easy so you can pursue a life that counts today—and for eternity. Those five mindsets are thankfulness, growth, opportunity, the big picture, and perseverance.

The thankfulness mindset helps you see the good amidst the bad. The growth mindset helps you close the gap between you and your dreams. The opportunity mindset enables you to unearth possibilities within your problems. The big picture mindset helps you take a few steps back to see how God is at work in your circumstances. And the perseverance mindset enables you to keep moving with a clear purpose and a sustainable pace.

When you develop all five mindsets, you'll be equipped with the attitude you need to run after a life of significance. Our lives follow our thinking, so these five mindsets are the place to start. As you do, you'll start to see a life that counts, and you'll be ready to make the next trade-off—comfort for character. This trade-off will cultivate in you the maturity you need to support the work God wants to accomplish through you.

Part 2: Maturity

Trade Comfort for Character

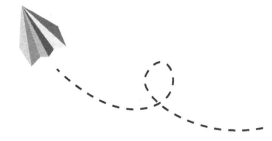

The first key to pursuing a life that counts is mindset, but the apostle Paul doesn't end there. As he continues his letter to the Philippians, he shifts his focus to the importance of mature character. Yes, our perspective is critical if we're going to stop chasing easy and pursue a life that counts. We have to see differently to achieve greatly. But for our achievements to endure, they must be built on the firm foundation of character. Without the bedrock of character, our lives will crack and crumble under the weight of our mission. Our character must mature in order to bear the fruit that is grown through the work of the Holy Spirit in our lives.

Author and pastor Andy Stanley defines character as, "the will to do what is right, as defined by God, regardless of personal cost."[36] Without the "will to do what is right," you'll always look for *easy* shortcuts. If "right" is defined by anyone but God, you'll tweak and modify the truth until it fits neatly into what's convenient in the moment. And if you only do what's right when the "personal cost" is low, it's only a matter of time before you put your character up for sale to the highest bidder.

Character compromises are common on Easy Street. Why? Because we're prone to the path of least resistance, and yet, resistance is what produces character. When our circumstances require perseverance, hard choices, and self-control, they create the perfect environment for our character to grow and mature.

The growth of your character can also take a hit on the road to success. When you work hard to achieve something big, you can find yourself on top of the mountain. That's a great feeling. The problem is, character rarely grows on mountaintops. The oxygen of humility is thin the higher up you go, and it's easy to think your current level of character will sustain you. But at the top of the mountain, we're more susceptible to pride, and therefore, we can become reckless with the disciplines that got us there in the first place.

Whether we're cruising down Easy Street or reaching the summit of success, it's tempting to think that we deserve a free pass. We entertain the subtle lie that tells us we deserve a break, a binge, or whatever form of comfort will satisfy us in the moment. But achieving a noble mission at the expense of your character is not a win. It's a short-term compromise that produces a long-term harvest of unintended consequences.

In this section, we'll walk through Philippians chapter two where we'll learn how to mature our character in five areas of life. Rather than focusing on *doing*, Paul turns our attention to *being*. What kind of firm, unwavering character does Paul call us to cultivate in place of comfort?

- Love
- Humble Service
- Obedience
- Trust
- Honor

Each one of these characteristics marks a mature life, and a life that counts. Character is not a school, a course, or a degree that you complete in a week, a semester, or a year. In fact, character has no graduation date. Building character is a lifelong process of sowing the right kind of seeds in order to produce an abundant harvest of mature fruit inside of you. Without making a commitment to mature your character, you'll never make your life count today—or for eternity. Let's start the maturing process now.

Chapter 6
Love
Un-Bankrupt Your Character

William Raspberry, a Pulitzer Prize winning journalist, once gave some outstanding advice to young leaders. He said, "If you want to be thought of as a solid, reliable pillar of your community when you're fifty, you can't be an irresponsible, corner-cutting exploiter at twenty-five... The time to worry about your reputation is before you have one. You determine your reputation by deciding who and what you are and by keeping that lofty vision for yourself in mind, even when you're having a rip-roaring good time."[37]

Author Ruth Haley Barton offers some similar advice when she says, "We set young leaders up for a fall if we encourage them to envision what they can do before they consider the kind of person they should be."[38]

Whether you're young, old, or somewhere in between, character is at the heart of a life that counts. Without it, everything you work hard to build will eventually collapse. So, what character qualities mark the life of someone who has abandoned Easy Street in pursuit of a life of meaning and purpose? That's the focus of Philippians chapter two, and the first trait on Paul's list is the greatest virtue of all: Love.

Love tops Paul's character list when he writes, "If you've gotten anything at all out of following Christ, *if his love has made any difference in your life*, if being in a community of the Spirit means anything to you, if you have a heart, if you *care*—then do me a favor: Agree with each other, *love each other*, be deep-spirited friends" (Philippians 2:1-2,

MSG, emphasis added). Paul's instructions are clear—if Christ's love has changed you, let His love flow through you.

Bankrupt Without Love

I like to get things done. I start each day at zero, and deep within me there's a desire to accomplish *something*, whether it's making progress on a project at work, cleaning out the garage at home, or writing a few paragraphs in this book. While this trait is a great asset when it comes to delivering results, it can also distract me if I don't manage it correctly. Simply put: my vision for *results* can hijack my value for *relationships*.

I believe Paul understood this tension between results and relationships. He was driven by a mission to preach the Gospel, but his letters often open with heartfelt greetings that reveal his love for people. In addition to his focus on love in Philippians, he also powerfully described the nature of love in his first letter to the church in Corinth. In chapter 12, he describes a wide variety of spiritual gifts that the Holy Spirit has imparted to the church. Then, in chapter 14, Paul describes the proper use of these gifts. Interestingly, wedged between chapter 12 and chapter 14 is the "love chapter." Paul writes:

> *"If I speak with human eloquence and angelic ecstasy but don't love, I'm nothing but the creaking of a rusty gate. If I speak God's Word with power, revealing all his mysteries and making everything plain as day, and if I have faith that says to a mountain, 'Jump,' and it jumps, but I don't love, I'm nothing. If I give everything I own to the poor and even go to the stake to be burned as a martyr, but I don't love, I've gotten nowhere. So, no matter what I say, what I believe, and what I do, I'm bankrupt without love" (1 Corinthians 13:1-3, MSG).*

Have you ever been called a "creaking…rusty gate"? Have your efforts ever been compared to getting you "nothing" and "nowhere"? That's what a life without love produces. The last part of verse three is particularly convicting: "no matter what I say, what I believe, and what I do, I'm bankrupt without love." Consider the ramifications of those three statements.

1. No Matter What I Say

Have you ever heard someone proclaim with conviction how much we should love one another, but when you take a quick look at their rants on social media you discover that their love is *selective* at best? Like a cafeteria line where you choose *a little bit of this* and *a little bit of that*, their love has been demoted to nothing more than a megaphone for personal preferences.

Bob Goff, author of the best-selling book *Love Does*, has included his cell phone number in the back of his book. Every day he gets dozens and dozens of phone calls from total strangers, and as he talks with each one, he exudes genuine love and compassion. A few years ago, I watched an interview with Bob Goff where he mentioned that every couple of weeks he gets a phone call from a guy who cusses him out. He said he had no idea who the man is, or what the man was so angry about, but Bob refused to hang up on him. He didn't retaliate with his words, but instead exhibited sincere, consistent love.[39] Why? Because Bob's heart isn't bankrupt. His account is filled with authentic love, and each day he makes withdrawals that he can shower onto the people around him.

> *I'm not asking you to compromise your beliefs—that will only create its own set of problems. But I am challenging you to hold and express your beliefs in a spirit of love.*

2. No Matter What I Believe

Having clear convictions and beliefs is very important. Without them, we can be tossed about by deceptive doctrines and philosophies. However, the *spirit* in which we hold our beliefs is also important. I'm concerned when I see people in the body of Christ who use their beliefs to demean, shame, or attack others. That act does nothing more than burn bridges, weaken the body, destroy unity, and undermine the testimony of the Gospel.

Please hear me: I'm not asking you to compromise your beliefs—that will only create its own set of problems. But I am challenging you to hold and express your beliefs in a spirit of love. Again, Paul said, "*No matter...what I believe...I'm bankrupt without love.*"

On one occasion, John came to Jesus and said, "Teacher, we saw someone using your name to cast out demons, but we told him to stop because he wasn't in our group." (Mark 9:38). Every time I read that verse I chuckle, because it sounds like so many petty arguments we hear today.

How did Jesus respond?

"Don't stop him!" Jesus said. "No one who performs a miracle in my name will soon be able to speak evil of me. *Anyone who is not against us is for us*" (Mark 9:39-40, emphasis added).

If we have the same outlook as Jesus, I'm guessing we'll fight a whole lot less and love a whole lot more, and reach many more people with the Gospel. John Maxwell has often said that if you want to reach people, you have to start *connecting* with them, and stop *correcting* them. Love starts with connecting.

I don't believe it's an accident that in the same passage in Philippians Two where Paul said, "love each other," he also said, "agree with each other," and "be deep-spirited friends." Love is what gives your beliefs the ability to garner respect and transform lives.

3. No Matter What I Do

Consider the implications of Paul's words to the Corinthians: "If I give everything I own to the poor and even go to the stake to be burned as a martyr, but I don't love, I've gotten nowhere." Simply put, you can actually perform loving acts *without* love.

Today people stand up for the rights of others, working hard to right the injustices that harm the innocent and the powerless. That is a noble act. We need more people standing up for the voiceless and the helpless. But I've also discovered a disheartening trend among so many ambassadors of justice—not only do they hate the injustice, but they hate the perpetrator of injustice. Have you ever stopped to consider the hypocrisy of advocating for justice while simultaneously hating people? We can still love people without condoning their senseless and sinful acts.

> *Do acts of love, but also be a loving person. Don't love selectively; love unconditionally.*

Paul tells us that true love is patient and kind. True love is not jealous, boastful, proud, or rude. True love isn't irritable, doesn't demand its way, and doesn't keep a record of wrong. Love doesn't rejoice about injustice, but instead, rejoices when truth wins. Love doesn't give up or lose faith, but instead remains hopeful and endures through every circumstance.[40] No matter what I do, without *this kind of love*, I'm bankrupt.

I'm not suggesting that you endorse the unjust acts of people who are hurting and oppressing the poor and the innocent. This behavior is evil, and we cannot ignore evil. Instead, we must overcome evil with good.[41] Do acts of love, but also *be* a loving person. Don't love selectively; love unconditionally. Paul's point is clear: labor without love is useless. You can labor with your gifts and abilities all day long, but when your labor is void of love, your gifts become weapons. What was meant to help others actually hurts them instead. Love is meant to fuel your gifts.

No matter what I *say*, *believe*, or *do*, without love, I am utterly bankrupt. Without love, our intelligence, skills, expertise, and degrees don't mean much to anyone, including God. Without love, my passionate speech and my deep-rooted beliefs will fail to reach their greatest impact. Resist that dark road void of love. Stop chasing easy and trade up to undefiled love.

Love Isn't Easy

I'm always amazed, and inspired, by the constant love of elderly couples who have faithfully loved one another for 50, 60, even 70 years or more. What started as a young, flirtatious love blossomed into a mature, unconditional love that has weathered the ups and downs of life. This love is often seen in new dimensions as older partners care for their ailing spouses, not just during a bout with the flu, but when crippling disease sets into their body. This love is rich beyond measure.

Several years ago, Karen and I got a very *small* taste of the energy and commitment this type of love requires. After my heart surgery, Karen loved me in the deepest and most compassionate ways during my six-week recovery. She rallied prayer support, helped me with medications, drove me to doctor appointments and rehab sessions, listened to my reflections, and tended to a never-ending list of details to make sure I had what I needed to fully recover.

A couple of years later, I would return the favor.

One evening, when we were at Karen's parents' home, Karen was walking down the stairs toward the living room when she suddenly missed a step and tumbled to the bottom of the staircase. She was in obvious pain, and it became apparent that we needed to call for an ambulance.

When the paramedics arrived, they loaded Karen into an ambulance and began administering pain medication. At first, we thought she had severely twisted her knee. We later discovered that Karen had torn her ACL, broken her tibia, and torn her meniscus. Needless to say, the recovery would be long and painful.

After several weeks, she finally returned to the school where she worked as a counselor. Her injury prevented her from driving, so I would take her to work each morning, help her into a wheelchair, and wheel her down the hallway to her office. Each morning we would pass the same group of teenagers, and each afternoon I would return to the school to pick her up.

One student later asked Karen, "Is that your husband who brings you each morning?" "Yes!" Karen said. Then the young man replied, "That's a *real* man."

Real man?

Pushing your wife in a wheelchair makes you a real man?

It certainly doesn't feel heroic to me, but to a struggling teenager who had rarely seen love in action, the smallest act of love captured his attention.

Through both of these circumstances—my heart failure and Karen's broken knee—we learned the systems and routines necessary to make the recovery more bearable for each other. It wasn't uncommon to spend a couple of hours each morning, and a couple of hours each evening, helping one another get ready for the day or wind down for the evening. But that's the nature of love.

> *A very real part of true love is **beautifully boring**. It's routine. It's the litany of small, faithful, unseen acts of tender love.*

Love isn't an endless string of romantic encounters and happy feelings. Yes, there are plenty of those wonderful moments too, and I'm so grateful for each one of them. But a very real part of true love is *beautifully boring*. It's routine. It's the litany of small, faithful, unseen acts of tender love. In those moments, love isn't easy, but it is authentic and real.

If you want to leave a legacy worth remembering when you die, you have to write a legacy worth recording while you're alive. Such a legacy is written with the ink of love; that's what people remember and celebrate.

Making Love Personal

What does it look like to live an "un-bankrupt" life, full of God's unconditional love? It requires us to make love personal. First John 3:16-17 says, "We know what real love is because Jesus gave up his life for us. So we also ought to give up our lives for our brothers and sisters. If someone has enough money to live well and sees a brother or sister in need but shows no compassion—how can God's love be in that person?"

Notice the *personal* nature of love in this passage. John said to love our *brothers* and *sisters*. That's *plural*. In other words, we should love *everybody*. But then, in verse 17, he challenged us to share with our *brother* and *sister* in need. That's *singular*. That's *personal*. A blanket kind of love (for all) is sometimes easier to swallow than a personal kind of love (for one). As Eric Hoffer once said, "It is easier to love humanity as a whole than to love one's neighbor."[42] In other words, saying "love everybody" is easier than saying, "love your overbearing friend," or "love your obnoxious neighbor," or "love your rude cousin," or "love your narcissistic boss." When your love moves from plural to singular, you put a personal face on the recipient of your love. That's how you can make love count today.

God didn't call us to chase the easy kind of love—the kind that's here today but gone when the price tag gets too high. He has called us to *be loving*. Let your character start here. Let it mature with roots grounded in love. This is the kind of love that you won't find on Easy Street, but it's worth trading up for. Agree with each other, love each other, and be deep-spirited friends. Un-bankrupt your character by filling it with a love that's personal, practical, and unconditional.

Chapter 7
Humble Service
Develop "Step Aside/Set Aside" Character

One overwhelming desire sits front and center on Easy Street: the desire to be served. The focus isn't what I *could* do for you, but rather, what you *should* do for me. There's a not-so subtle entitlement that sets in on Easy Street as we create our list of expectations, perks, and privileges. Ultimately, it's all about me.

There's just one problem.

This focus on "me" gets in the way of living a life that counts.

If your character is going to mature beyond Easy Street, you're going to have to shift your focus beyond yourself. You'll need to become community-focused, and that starts when you commit to do something for someone else.

Have you ever worked frantically to get something done while everyone else was on a coffee break? Have you ever bent over backward to get the house cleaned while your kids sat on the couch watching TV? Have you ever unpacked boxes for your new apartment while your roommate sat on the floor playing video games? At some point, you probably said with exasperation, "Well, don't just sit there...*do something.*"

In many ways we live in a *sit there* culture rather than a *do something* culture. "Sit there" is all about *consuming*, but "do something" is all about *contributing*. One has a "be served" focus, while the other has a "serve others" focus.

As Paul continues his letter to the Philippians, he dives deep into this character shift from being served to serving others. Paul writes,

"Don't push your way to the front; don't sweet-talk your way to the top. Put yourself aside, and help others get ahead. Don't be obsessed with getting your own advantage. Forget yourselves long enough to lend a helping hand" (Philippians 2:3-4, MSG). Paul's "other-focused" attitude offers us a powerful truth: you do something for someone else when you *step aside* and *set aside*.

> **Paul's "other-focused" attitude offers us a powerful truth: you do something for someone else when you step aside and set aside.**

What does it mean to *step aside* and *set aside*? We find the answer when Paul points to the example of Jesus. He gives us two practical ways to move from being served to serving others. Let's first talk about what it means to "step aside."

Step Aside So Others Can Step Ahead

Two attitudes dominate our culture—a *selfish mindset* and a *scarcity mindset*. The selfish mindset is all about *what* I can get, but the scarcity mindset is all about *how much* I can get. The selfish mindset is all about *me*, but the scarcity mindset is all about *more*.

You can probably recall the selfish and scarcity mindsets from your childhood in moments such as when you and your friends went out for pizza. You had to act fast if you wanted to get your fair share. The reasoning went like this:

"There's only *eight* slices. I better fight for *my* slice, because if someone else gets my slice, then we'll run out of pizza, and I'll go hungry. Besides, there probably aren't any more ingredients in the kitchen to make another pizza. In fact, this might be the last pizza ever to be made."

I know, it sounds irrational (perhaps even comical), but that's how we think when our mindset is focused on *me* and *more*. Unfortunately, it doesn't end with pizza. "Me" and "more" cast dark shadows over everything from the classroom to the boardroom, from the shopping mall to the halls of power. As a result, our sinful appetites get the best of us.

What's the cure?

Humble service.

Look again at Paul's words in Philippians 2:3-4: "Don't push your way to the front; don't sweet-talk your way to the top. *Put yourself aside, and help others get ahead.* Don't be obsessed with getting your own advantage. Forget yourselves long enough to lend a helping hand" (MSG, emphasis added).

When I think of stepping aside so others can step ahead, I think about opening a door for somebody else. When you walk up to a door with your spouse, a friend, or a co-worker, or even a complete stranger, a common courtesy is to open the door for them. In other words, you're stepping aside so someone else can step ahead. That same principle is also true in other areas of life.

What would happen if you opened the door to God's work by praying for somebody else? What would happen if you opened the door to a new job by introducing a friend to your boss? Every time you do something for somebody else, you are opening a door for them. It might be a spiritual door, relational door, financial door, or professional door. Why is this important? There are two reasons: first, when you step aside so others can step ahead, it helps them reach their full potential. And second, it helps you live and lead with pure motives.

Set Aside Status for Service

Being a servant doesn't end when you step aside so others can step ahead. Paul continues his servant-minded challenge when he writes:

> *"Think of yourselves the way Christ Jesus thought of himself. He had equal status with God but didn't think so much of himself that he had to cling to the advantages of that status no matter what. Not at all. When the time came, he set aside the privileges of deity and took on the status of a slave, became* human*! Having become human, he stayed human. It was an incredibly humbling process. He didn't claim special privileges. Instead, he lived a selfless, obedient life and then died a selfless, obedient death—and the worst kind of death at that—a crucifixion"* (Philippians 2:5-8, MSG).

Notice that phrase, "he set aside the privileges of deity." Jesus, the Son of God, didn't dip his toe in the pool of humanity and then jump back to heaven and say, "No thanks, I'll stay here where I can enjoy my perks and privileges." Instead, He became human and fully embraced

His mission, setting aside status for service.

True service requires humility. As Paul said, for Jesus to give up heaven for humanity was, "an incredibly humbling process." That spirit of humility was not only evident in Jesus' death, but also in His life. For example, when Jesus washed his disciples' feet, John said, "He got up from the table" (John 13:4). That's the first step to service. We have to push away from the table of comfort where we sit. We have to humbly assume the posture of a servant.

After Jesus washed the feet of His disciples, He challenged them with these words: "I have given you an example to follow. Do as I have done to you" (John 13:15). Jesus not only *modeled* serving, but He gave us a *mandate* to serve others. Then He said, "Now that you know these things, God will bless you for doing them" (John 13:17). Most people believe the key to blessing is to focus on getting. Jesus took a paradoxical approach: the key to blessing is to start giving.

> **People who spend their lives in constant pursuit of "me" and "more" are never satisfied. They never experience peace or contentment.**

In this way, Jesus has shown us that service is a blessing. I discovered a long time ago that the happiest people on earth are those who serve. People who spend their lives in constant pursuit of "me" and "more" are never satisfied. They never experience peace or contentment. The key to happiness is to learn to *step aside* and *set aside*. That's what it looks like to trade comfort for character. That's what it means to stop chasing easy and pursue a life that counts today—and for eternity.

Instead of Service to Myself...

At the age of 18, Scott Harrison left the Christian home he grew up in to move to New York with his band. One month later his band broke up, and Scott began a ten-year climb up the social nightlife ladder in New York City. When he reached the top, he was a picture of success. He drove a BMW, wore a Rolex, lived in a nice apartment in New York, and had a girlfriend on the cover of magazines. But with his success came every vice his nightlife had to offer. He smoked two packs of cigarettes a day, and he picked up habits like gambling, pornography, strip clubs, cocaine, ecstasy, and marijuana.[43]

Scott had become spiritually, morally, and emotionally bankrupt. Reflecting back on his life, he said, "My body was dulling. My conscience was cooked. I couldn't remember the last time I'd laughed without being high or cried about losing someone or something important to me. I couldn't remember the last time I'd prayed. It took about ten years to pull it off, but somehow I'd managed to become the worst version of myself."[44] Despite what his life had become, Scott's parents never stopped praying for him.

While on a trip to South America, Scott came to a humbling realization—if he continued down the path he was on, his tombstone would read, "Here lies a man who has gotten a million people wasted over the course of his life." That stark awakening started Scott on a journey of spiritual renewal.

He began reading the Bible, as well as books by A.W. Tozer. With every page, he learned about the love of God. Scott said, "I felt like Tozer was speaking directly to me when he spoke of the danger of hungering for material possessions."[45] In his reading, Scott was being confronted by a life opposite to what his life had become. He returned to New York and began asking, "Instead of service to myself, what would it look like to help others?"[46] Along with this question, a verse from James kept popping in his mind: "Pure religion is this. Look after orphans and widows in their distress, and keep yourself from being polluted by the world" (James 1:27).[47]

> **Instead of service to myself, what would it look like to help others?**

Six months later, Scott took a radical step of obedience. He sold almost everything he owned and gave one year of his life to Mercy Ships. Mercy Ships is a humanitarian organization that provides free life-saving surgeries in places where medical care is almost non-existent. Over 100,000 surgeries have been performed on Mercy Ships since 1978.[48] The moment Scott stepped onto the ship, he gave up all his vices; he never smoked, gambled, looked at pornography, or stepped into a strip club again, and he remained celibate for over five years until his wedding night.

Mercy Ships sailed a 500-foot hospital down the coast of Africa. To Scott's utter surprise, over 5,000 people were awaiting their arrival when they pulled into a harbor in Liberia, and yet only 1,500 surgery slots were available. Dr. Gary Parker—the ship's chief medical officer—said to the team, "There are more than five thousand people outside. Every single one deserves our attention and kindness. Look them in the eye. Provide them with first-rate health care. Try not to be overwhelmed by the numbers. Focus on the human being in front of you and how you can help them. Let's pray."[49] They would need God's help for the mammoth mission in front of them. Some patients had walked for over a month, desperate for medical care.

Over the course of that year, Scott began to love people like he never had before, many of whom who were sick, hurting, and scorned by their communities. He took more than 50,000 photos, documenting the stories of countless lives saved, and every few days he would blast some of his photos to his "Club List" of 15,000 people, challenging them to give to the mission of Mercy Ships. Many people unsubscribed, but others started to give.

During a second year with Mercy Ships, Scott's desire to make a difference continued to grow, but there were many needs and he wasn't sure where to start. At one point, Dr. Parker told him, "Scott, rather than five or ten different issues, perhaps God wants you to focus on one intensely. Pick that one issue carefully."[50] The one issue he couldn't shake was dirty water. Every day, 785 million people (one-tenth of the planet's population), drink dirty water, which is the cause of 52% of all disease in the developing world.[51] This would become the focus of Scott's mission.

When he returned to New York, Scott started a non-profit organization called "Charity: Water." At that point, Scott had given away all his money and was completely broke. He crashed at the loft of an old club friend, and used this friend's couch as his first office. Struggling to raise money, Scott came up with an idea. He decided to throw a party on his birthday in a local nightclub. His strategy was simple—lure people in with an open bar and charge $20 when they entered. More than 700 people showed up, and Scott raised $15,000, which he used to provide water to a refugee camp in Northern Uganda. Then he sent photos back to the 700 people who attended the party.

Scott's efforts started gaining traction, and he began to challenge people to donate their birthdays, asking for their age in dollars. One 7-year-old kid in Austin, Texas knocked on doors asking for $7.00

donations and raised $22,000. An 89-year-old gave up her birthday, saying, "I'm turning 89 and I want to make that possible for more people in Africa." Another man donated the $10,000 that he had saved up for an engagement ring. He and his fiancé were determined to start their marriage with a radical act of generosity.[52]

As of this writing, over half a billion dollars has been raised for Charity: Water. They've funded over 78,000 water projects which serve over thirteen million people in 29 countries.[53] Scott has no intention of slowing down anytime soon. He is inspired often by the words of Avot De Rabbi Natan: "Do not be afraid of work that has no end."

> **Author John Dickson defines humility as, "the noble choice to forgo your status, deploy your resources or use your influence for the good of others before yourself...the humble person is marked by a willingness to hold power in service of others.**

This amazing charity work began when Scott confronted what his life had become, and then he was forced to wrestle with a question: "Instead of service to myself, what would it look like to help others?"

Scott chose to step aside so millions of others could step ahead with clean water. Scott chose to set aside the status that accompanied his nightlife ambitions and pursued a life that counts through humble service.

What about you?

What would happen if you stopped chasing Easy Street? What could happen if you stepped aside—by practicing humble service—so others could step ahead?

Putting the "Humble" in "Service"

Author John Dickson defines humility as, "the noble choice to forgo your status, deploy your resources or use your influence for the good of others before yourself...the humble person is marked by a willingness to hold power in service of others."[54] In other words, step aside so others can step ahead. Set aside status for service. This, as Dickson notes, is a "noble choice."

When we fail to make that noble choice, this pride comes with a price tag. Proverbs 16:18 says, "Pride goes before destruction, and haughtiness before a fall." But when we embrace humility as the posture for service, a different outcome ensues. For Jesus, Paul described that outcome with these words: "Because of that obedience, God lifted him high and honored him far beyond anyone or anything, ever, so that all created beings in heaven and on earth—even those long ago dead and buried—will bow in worship before this Jesus Christ, and call out in praise that he is the Master of all, to the glorious honor of God the Father" (Philippians 2:9-11, MSG). And for followers of Jesus, the apostle Peter said, "So humble yourselves under the mighty power of God, and at the right time he will lift you up in honor" (1 Peter 5:6). Simply put, pride is the elevated path that in the end is brought low; humility is the low path that in the end is elevated.

We can only serve effectively when we identify our gifts and then deploy them in service to others. However, always keep in mind that the spirit in which we use our gifts matters as much (if not more) than the gift itself. Our gifts are just that...*gifts*. They are not gods. When we turn a gift into a god, we diminish our reliance on God and become self-idolaters, blinded by our own pride. R.C. Sproul once said, "The grand difference between a human being and a supreme being is precisely this: Apart from God, I cannot exist. Apart from me, God does exist. God does not need me in order for Him to be; I do need God in order for me to be."[55] The quicker we learn this life lesson, the sooner we will experience God's grace.[56]

A life that counts is a life of service. It's one that steers clear of Easy Street and makes an intentional investment in others through the gifts and abilities God has entrusted to us. It's committed to step aside so others can step ahead, all out of a spirit of humility. Service and humility are signs of mature character.

Chapter 8
Obedience
Cultivate Character that's "All-In" and "Awe-Inspired"

It was the spring of 2014, and Stephen and Priscilla Perumalla were sitting in a missions conference at their church, listening to a church planter share his story. As the story unfolded, Priscilla leaned over to Stephen and whispered, "Doesn't this make you want to plant a church?" Stephen's initial response was, "Absolutely not!"

At the time, the Perumallas were youth pastors at a great church in Texas. They enjoyed living near family, and life was going pretty well. Moving wasn't anywhere on their radar. But God has a way of disrupting our comfort zones and putting a dream in our hearts for something new—something hard. For Stephen and Priscilla, He started stirring their hearts to plant a church from scratch in New York City.

That decision didn't come without a fight. Spiritual warfare was about to heat up to a degree the Perumallas had never known before. Anytime you decide to step out of the familiarity of Easy Street to start a church in a highly unchurched environment, the devil takes notice.

Shortly after saying "Yes" to God's call, Stephen became alarmed because he was beginning to have some physical challenges. At first, he kept quiet, hoping the symptoms would go away. The last thing he wanted to do was scare Priscilla and their two kids. But nothing changed, and a few weeks later he told Priscilla, and then scheduled an appointment with a urologist. The urologist believed it was an infection and put Stephen on six weeks of antibiotics. Again, nothing changed.

That's when Stephen was diagnosed with testicular cancer.

He was devastated.

Uncertainty gripped Stephen's heart as questions flooded his mind. Will we be able to move to New York City? Will I see my son graduate high school? Will I walk my daughter down the aisle? The questions were endless, and the fear was relentless.

They made a bold decision: "Cancer was not going to determine the timeline of our call.

In October 2014, Stephen had surgery, and because the cancer had not spread, he didn't have to undergo chemotherapy. At the same time, he began to doubt the timing of the family's move to New York City (and even the call to move at all). "Maybe we didn't hear God," Stephen thought, or "Maybe this is the wrong timing."

But as the questions rolled around in his head, something powerful rose up in his spirit. Something louder than the cancer. Something louder than the fear, doubt, and feelings of uncertainty. Something that spoke into the unknown and anchored Stephen and Priscilla to their God-given call. They made a bold decision: "Cancer was not going to determine the timeline of our call."

God knew about the cancer before Stephen did, and yet He still chose to call the Perumallas to New York City, so they stuck to their plan. Leaving behind a 1,600 square foot house, they moved to Upper Manhattan on July 5, 2015 and settled in a 500-square-foot apartment.

Their first year was spent acclimating to the city and building a core team to help plant the church. The Perumallas quickly realized that this endeavor was going to be a lot harder than they originally envisioned. Stephen said, "There's a reason that 95% of Manhattanites are unchurched. We had a steep hill to climb, but we were excited about the challenge." A family from Texas joined them in the journey, the team slowly came together, and an official launch date was set: September 18, 2016.

Three months before the launch of Grace Place NYC, Stephen went for a routine check-up with his doctor, expecting a great report. A few days later, the doctor called.

"Steve," he said. "I have bad news. Cancer has come back in one of your lymph nodes and you're going to have to have chemotherapy."

It was like a punch to the gut. "How could this happen?" Stephen thought. "Why would God allow this to happen again with the launch of our church so quickly approaching?"

After the initial shock, Stephen and Priscilla became convinced that God was going to perform a miracle, and that they would be able to share His miracle at their launch service to a packed school auditorium. They pushed chemotherapy as long as possible, making room for God to show up with an undeniable miracle. Stephen even went on an intense sugar free, cancer fighting diet (which he admits may have been harder than chemo).

Time was running out, so they asked the doctor to do another CT scan to see if the cancer was gone. Sitting in the doctor's office, Stephen and Priscilla were eager to hear the results. They fully expected the doctor to walk in and say, "I don't know how this happened, but the cancer is gone." With that single sentence, the Perumallas would then lead all of the doctors to Jesus. News would spread, revival would hit, and the church would be packed on opening day.

But nothing changed.

The scan came back with the same report: cancer. Priscilla admitted, "I had never been more disappointed with God than at that moment." With disbelief she said, "God, you sent us here and you called us here. What are you doing?"

Have you ever had one of those days (or one of those years)? "God, what are you thinking? What are you doing? Where are you?" You try your very best to trust Him, to walk faithfully with Him, but you wake up each day to silence. No answers. No breakthrough. No miracle. In those moments, it's easy to doubt God.

As they left the doctor's office, discouraged and disappointed with the news, they sat down on a bench outside of Gotham Café in the Upper East Side of Manhattan. Tears streamed down their faces as the reality of what they had just heard set in. Then Priscilla leaned over to Stephen and whispered, "Let's just worship."

They worshiped, prayed, and cried. Just like the Prophet Isaiah declared, with every breath of praise, the spirit of heaviness began to lift (Isaiah 61:3). Stephen said, "On that bench that day, we decided once again that cancer was not going to determine the timeline of God's call on our lives."

Launch Day

In August of 2016, one month before the launch of Grace Place NYC, Stephen started his first of four chemotherapy treatments at Memorial Sloan Kettering Cancer Center. A few weeks later, on September 18, Grace Place NYC launched with 82 people. Although chemotherapy was taking its toll, Stephen and Priscilla were encouraged by the turnout. But the excitement quickly faded. The very next week only 13 people showed up. Stephen couldn't even attend because he had to be hospitalized that week for life threatening complications with the chemo treatment. And in the four months that followed, there were some scary moments where death seemed to lurk at the doorstep. But time and again, God proved faithful.

Today, Stephen is cancer free, and he and Priscilla are leading a life-giving church in New York City. He's passionate about sharing the Gospel and introducing people to a transforming relationship with Jesus. They're making their lives count by advancing a mission to serve their city. Through all the hardship and the suffering, they've learned what it means to be *faithful*. In Stephen's words: "I'm convinced that the churches that 'make it' aren't led by the most talented pastors, but by men and women who simply decide to get back up when they get knocked down. In our journey, obedience to God became the light that led our path when darkness tried to overwhelm us…When I get to heaven, there is nothing I want to hear more than, 'Well done my good and faithful servant.'"[57]

All of us create timelines for the things we want. The problem is, we impose our timelines onto God's plan.

All of us create timelines for the things we want. The problem is, we impose our timelines onto God's plan. Stephen and Priscilla learned firsthand that God's timeline doesn't always match their wants, and yet they chose *obedience*, even when His timeline didn't make sense.

Obedience isn't defined by convenience. Obedience isn't dependent on logic or rationale. Obedience moves even when Easy Street mails a glittery invitation to return safely home. But look again at Stephen's courageous words: "Obedience to God became the light that led our path when darkness tried to overwhelm us." It's easy to obey in the light, but it's in the darkest hours that the beauty of "all-in" and "awe-inspired" obedience rings the loudest.

Awe-Inspired Obedience

What comes to your mind when you hear the word "obedient"? Do you think of a long list of constricting rules, a carefully crafted book of dos and don'ts? Do you think of your parents' unrealistic demands from your childhood? Do you think of a safe, predictable, goody two-shoes path where all the "perfect people" walk?

While obedience is a good trait, too often we view it through a bad lens. Rather than embracing the transformation it can produce in our lives, we focus on the things it will cost us and all of the things we give up. But what if I told you that obedience is not only good but *beautiful*? What if I told you that obedience is awe-inspiring?

In Philippians 2:12-18, Paul continues his emphasis on character by focusing on the awe-inspiring nature of obedience. He begins, "Dear friends, you always followed my instructions when I was with you. And now that I am away, it is even more important. Work hard to show the results of your salvation, *obeying God* with deep reverence and fear" (Philippians 2:12, emphasis added). Notice, Paul applauds the Philippians' obedience when he said, "you always followed my instructions." Now he is imploring them to continue their obedience, even in his absence.

When you read this verse, you might be reminded of childhood moments when you *had to obey* your parents and teachers. Maybe you didn't want to obey, but their presence was like a hawk that hovered over you. They told you to clean your room, or do an assignment, and then they looked over your shoulder to make sure you obeyed.

But what happened when your parents left you alone? You went right back to playing video games. What happened when your teacher stepped out of the classroom? You turned around and started talking to your friends. In other words, your obedience was determined by whether or not they were *present*. An absence of their presence turned into an absence of obedience.

When Paul writes his letter, he's saying, "Whether I'm with you or not—whether I'm in your city or not—*choose to obey*." The Amplified version describes it beautifully: "So then, my dear ones, just as you have always obeyed [my instructions with enthusiasm], not only in my presence, but now much more in my absence, continue to work out your salvation [that is, cultivate it, bring it to full effect, actively pursue spiritual maturity] with *awe-inspired fear and trembling* [using serious caution and critical self-evaluation to avoid anything that might offend God or discredit the name of Christ]" (Philippians 2:12, AMP, emphasis added). Notice, maturity requires obedience, and true obedience is awe-inspired.

Do you view obedience as an inconvenience or as a beautiful expression of love and devotion to God?

The type of obedience Paul described wasn't driven by a list of rules and regulations. It wasn't an inconvenience or an irritation. It was shaped by "awe-inspired fear and trembling." There was a serious—and yet joy-filled—nature to obedience. There was a deep desire to honor God and avoid discrediting His name.

Do you have that same desire today? Does the thought of discrediting Christ's name make you tremble? Do you view obedience as an inconvenience or as a beautiful expression of love and devotion to God (even when you face hardships like Stephen and Priscilla did)? This viewpoint certainly isn't how I've always understood obedience, but it reminds me of the words of Jesus: "If you love me, you will obey my commands" (John 14:15, NCV). And John said, "Loving God means keeping his commandments" (1 John 5:3). In other words, obedience to God is evidence of your love for God. So, how do you develop this awe-inspired obedience in your life? It has two components: Fruit and Root.

The Fruit of Obedience

Jesus was pretty clear about the importance of a fruit-bearing life. *Everybody* bears fruit. Some fruit is good, some fruit is bad. In fact, when Jesus talked about bearing fruit, he said, "you can identify people by their actions" (Matthew 7:20). Simply put, the fruit of your life is evidence of your obedience to God. In Philippians 2:14-15, Paul gives us a taste of the fruit of obedience with two practical expressions: attitude and action.

1. Attitude

Paul says, "Do everything without complaining and arguing." Not some things. Not most things. *Everything.* Complaining and arguing are negative attitudes that cast dark shadows over our lives. We can quickly become like Alexander in the children's classic, *Alexander and the Terrible, Horrible, No Good, Very Bad Day*. Alexander has a terrible day filled with everything from getting gum in his hair to being demoted to "third best friend" status. But do you know what Alexander's real problem was? His attitude. His attitude, not his circumstances, was the dark shadow that defined his life.[58]

Paul gave us a similar recipe for a bad day—complaining and arguing. When we complain and argue, we let negativity darken our outlook. In that moment, it's easy to forget that our attitudes give people the very first taste of the fruit of our lives. In fact, people can taste your attitude the minute you walk into a room, even if you haven't spoken a word.

I like how John Maxwell describes attitude. He writes, "Attitude…It is the 'advance man' of our true selves. Its roots are inward but its fruit is outward. It is our best friend or our worst enemy. It is more honest and more consistent than our words. It is an outward look based on past experiences. It is a thing which draws people to us or repels them. It is never content until it is expressed. It is the librarian of our past. It is the speaker of our present. It is the prophet of our future."[59]

Obeying the Lord through our attitude is challenging when life is hard, which is why Paul's words have so much authority. Penning these words while sitting in prison, Paul had plenty to complain about. And yet he didn't. In verse 15 Paul keeps a productive attitude "…so that no one can criticize you." Paul understood that attitudes are amplifiers. When our attitudes turn negative with arguments and complaints, we amplify a poor testimony of the Gospel.

2. Action

The second expression of the fruit of obedience is our actions, everything from the words we speak to the way we behave. Paul concludes verse 15 with these words: "Live clean, innocent lives as children of God, shining like bright lights in a world full of crooked and perverse people." The way we live gives people a taste of who we are. Action reveals both character and integrity.

Paul implored his young apprentice Timothy with a similar challenge: "Be an example to all believers in what you say, in the way you live, in your love, your faith, and your purity" (1 Timothy 4:12). Look at the comprehensive nature of this verse. We should exemplify God-honoring action in our:

- Words ("what you say")
- Life ("the way you live")
- Relationships with Others ("in your love")
- Relationship with God ("your faith")
- Morals ("and your purity")

Like our attitudes, our actions also impact others. When we live clean and innocent lives, Paul says we are "shining like bright lights." You can't be a bright light if your character is inconsistent with how God has called you to live. Actions truly do speak louder than words.

Your *attitudes* and *actions* are the outward indicator of the fruit of obedience in your life. As our attitudes and actions mature, it reflects a life of obedience. But fruit doesn't come alone. It starts with a *Root*.

The Root of Obedience

We usually focus on the Fruit rather than the Root; after all, fruit is much easier to see. However, there is danger in focusing solely on the fruit: we can become consumed by human attempts at behavior modification. Keep in mind that the fruit is simply a by-product of the root. Paul defines the fruit of obedience—attitudes and actions—in verses 14 and 15, but he also describes the root of obedience in verses 13 and 16. The root is like the bookends of obedience.

Your attitudes and actions are the outward indicator of the fruit of obedience in your life. As our attitudes and actions mature, it reflects a life of obedience.

Paul starts (verse 13) and ends (verse 16) with the root, and the fruit is wedged in the middle (verses 14 and 15). The root of obedience includes two things.

1. The Activity of God's Spirit

The work of God's spirit in you feeds the fruit of obedience. Paul said it like this: "For God is working in you, giving you the desire and the power to do what pleases him" (Philippians 2:13). When we welcome the Holy Spirit's work inside of us, we experience the *desire* to please God and the *power* to please God. In other words, there is delight (rather than drudgery) in obeying God, and there is power to follow through.[60]

Stephen and Priscilla found the strength to obey God's call by cooperating with the Holy Spirit's timeline. God not only gave them the desire, but He also gave them His strength. They didn't just say "Yes" to God's initial call on their lives, they also said "Yes" to God's on-going activity in their lives.

How do we embrace God's work in our lives today? It starts by putting Him first and seeking Him first (Matthew 6:33). When Jesus said to "seek first his kingdom," He was saying to seek *first* the rule and reign of God, in and over your life. Not second. Not after you've tried everything else. Not according to your timeline. Not when you've run out of options and God is all

> **The fruit of your life is determined by what's first in your life.**

you have left. First! God must come first because the *fruit* of your life is determined by what's *first* in your life.

When bad fruit shows up in our lives, we often plead with God to give us different fruit. But the fruit's not the problem; it's a symptom. The real problem is in the root. That's why Solomon said, "Start with God—the first step in learning is bowing down to God; only fools thumb their noses at such wisdom and learning" (Proverbs 1:7, MSG).

Start with God by seeking Him first and welcoming the daily *activity* of His Spirit in your life. This is the first bookend to obedience. When you say yes to the activity of God's Spirit, He gives you the *desire* and *power* to obey.

2. The Anchor of God's Word

The second bookend of obedience is to be anchored to God's Word. Paul said, "Hold firmly to the word of life; then, on the day of Christ's return, I will be proud that I did not run the race in vain and that my work was not useless" (Philippians 2:16). Believe it or not, God's Word has extraordinary power to help you walk in obedience.

According to research by the Center for Bible Engagement, if a person engages the Bible four or more times per week, their lives look radically different than those who do not. "In fact, the lives of Christians who do not engage the Bible most days of the week are statistically the same as the lives of non-believers."[61] How impacting is "The Power of 4"? Somebody who engages the Bible four or more times per week is:

- 57% less likely to get drunk
- 68% less likely to have sex outside of marriage

- 61% less likely to view pornography
- 74% less likely to gamble
- 228% more likely to share their faith with others
- 231% more likely to disciple others
- 407% more likely to memorize Scripture[62]

Scripture is a powerful anchor. When you hold firmly to it, your attitudes and actions are shaped by its wisdom. In this way, scripture helps you grow the roots of a life that counts.

The activity of God's Spirit and the anchor of His Word are the bookends of obedience. When we welcome the Spirit's activity in our lives, and when we are anchored to His Word, our attitudes and actions are drawn toward obedience. The right root produces the right fruit. This is the evidence of spiritual maturity.

Paul concludes this passage with these words: "But I will rejoice even if I lose my life, pouring it out like a liquid offering to God, just like your faithful service is an offering to God. And I want all of you to share that joy. Yes, you should rejoice, and I will share your joy." (Philippians 2:17-18). Paul understood that sacrificial obedience is a joy, and regardless of the outcome, it's worth it.

Obedience isn't easy. Stephen and Priscilla learned that firsthand. If you're looking for the easy path, compromise is much less painful (at least in the short-term). But in the long-term, short-cuts come with a high price of unintended consequences.

Remember, character is greater than comfort every time. Abandon Easy Street and go "all in" with "awe-inspired" obedience. Don't leave obedience on a dark, dusty shelf in the garage of your life. Instead, pull it out, plant the seed, and let the root produce the fruit. That's how your character matures.

Chapter 9
Trust

Build Character on the Edge of the Diving Board

P eople will do just about anything to stay in their comfort zone; avoiding discomfort is some people's number one goal. However, your comfort zone requires no true trust in God. It's easy to trust God if my bank account is full, I'm physically healthy, I'm at the top of my career, and I'm madly in love. Trust? Who needs it when life is good, when life is *easy*? Self-dependence will work just fine.

The grandiose dream of Easy Street is to do nothing more than protect my own comfort. A life that counts, on the other hand, requires character, and the deep wells of mature character are formed by an equally deep trust in the Lord.

Stepping Off the Diving Board

When I was a kid, my Mom took me and my brothers and sister to a local swimming pool so we could learn how to swim. It was a rectangle shaped pool, with two diving boards at the end: the low dive and the high dive. The high dive was the crown jewel of the swimming experience. If you jumped off the high dive, you achieved the pinnacle of "kid success" in swimming class.

One day, toward the end of our swimming course, our instructor challenged us to make the jump. We had already jumped off the low dive time and time again, but none of us had ventured to the top of the high dive.

Determined to take the challenge, I climbed the ladder and walked to the end of the board. My toes clung to the edge of the board as I looked down at the water. I thought, "This looks a lot higher than it did from down below."

From where I stood, the water may as well have been a mile away. I was nervous, but there was no way I was going to turn around and descend the ladder of shame. So, I raised my hands above my head (just like my instructor had taught me), took a deep breath, and then I jumped. When I came up out of the water, I heard the sweet cheers of victory.

Mission accomplished.

From then on, jumping off the high dive became second nature.

Following God Off the End of the Diving Board

Swimming pools aren't the only places we experience diving boards in life. God often leads us to places that require us to step off the board of our security into the pool of the unknown. That step requires both faith and trust. It requires us to let go of "what is" and step into "what could be."

God leads us up the high dive and then He stands behind us and gently pushes us to jump. He's nudging, prodding, and speaking—inspiring us with a bold vision to leave what we know and jump into something new.

But fear taunts us.

Fear tells us that such a step is irrational, illogical, even foolish. Fear whispers lies that make us doubt ourselves. Fear tells us that God would never lead us to the edge of the board. After all, God wants me to play it safe, doesn't He? Safe is wise, right?

> *The same God that is pushing us to jump is in the water waiting for us to arrive. He's here, and He's there.*

As we look down, we can't even see the water. A fog of doubt and uncertainty has formed between us and the pool. For all we know, the fog could be hiding certain failure. But God keeps nudging us and calling us. He assures us that He will be faithful.

Here's the ironic part.

The same God that is pushing us to jump is in the water waiting for us to arrive.

He's *here*, and He's *there*.

The question is, do we trust Him?

God wants to lead you outside of your comfort zone, far from Easy Street, into a place that requires you to trust Him. He wants to deposit a dream inside of you that makes a difference today, and for eternity. That kind of dream cannot be achieved in your own strength, with your own resources, and in your own wisdom. And that kind of dream is only found when you let go of your safe today and choose His vision of tomorrow.

It's not easy.

It feels unsafe.

But isn't the will of God the safest place you can be?

Our Jump

The longer I live, the more convinced I am that life is one long journey of learning to trust God. Our willingness to trust was tested in 2012, when Karen and I jumped off the diving board to plant a church near downtown Fort Worth, Texas. We had served for years in a variety of local church and non-profit leadership roles, but starting a church was something entirely new.

In the years prior, Karen and I had dozens of conversations about the possibility of launching a new church. As time passed, I grew restless—ready to do something new—but Karen challenged me to finish school first. Both of us were working on our Masters degrees, and our daughter was preparing to graduate high school. Karen's wisdom rang loud and clear: "Let's all finish school before we take the next step." I'm glad I listened.

In September of 2011, God gave me three confirmations in a matter of two hours that it was time to pursue this dream. First, in a conversation with my friend, Jeff, we talked about the idea of planting a church. In that phone discussion, Jeff encouraged me and expressed belief in my dream.

Less than one hour later, I met with Derek, another friend. Interestingly, we weren't even supposed to meet that morning. Through a miscommunication of meeting times, Derek showed up that morning at Starbucks (where we normally met), and I happened to be there.

During our conversation, Derek spoke the same affirming words that Jeff had shared with me just a few minutes earlier. Both encouraged me in my exploration of church planting, and both addressed some of my hesitations and reservations. They challenged me to be unique and creative, and to leverage the strengths God gave me to plant a church that would match my God-given design and passions.

Finally, that same morning, as I drove from Starbucks to the church where I was working at the time, my mom called me. She told me that the previous night during her prayer meeting, one of her friends began to pray for me. As she did, she spoke a prophetic word, describing my life like a flower blooming in the desert. Her words came from Isaiah 35:1: "Even the wilderness and desert will rejoice in those days; the desert will blossom with flowers" (TLB). I was in awe that in only two hours God spoke clearly through three different people about our future.

For nearly three years, I had regularly prayed a seven-word prayer: "God, how do you transform a city?" I wasn't naïve enough to believe that a single church would change an entire city without help from anyone else, but that question would not go away.

Then, on September 16, 2011, as I was praying at home about this possibility of church planting, the Holy Spirit prompted me to sit down at my computer and write the vision for a new church. On that day, I was overcome with emotion. As tears streamed down my face, I typed these words:

> "I Dream of a Church. I dream of a church that inspires community. A place where people do not stand alone but are united by the common ground of the cross of Christ. I dream of a community of Christ followers who experience life transformed by Christ and are committed to loving God and loving each other. I dream of a church where every person discovers their purpose in life. I dream of people owning their personal growth and aggressively growing to their full, God-given capacity, so that their God-given purpose may be fully realized. I dream of a church that plants seeds on fertile ground and reap a harvest beyond the wildest dreams of the planter and the one being harvested. I dream of a church that influences culture. I dream of people leveraging their life purpose to assume leadership in the community, their career, the church, and in God-ordained causes to redeem that which is broken. I dream of young

*leaders and established leaders shaping society with the Gospel
and redeeming business, media, arts, and education, to their
God-intended design. I dream of a church that plays offense
and innovates solutions to the problems of our world. I dream
of a church that changes cities."*

I typed these exact words as fast as I could, sensing that the Holy
Spirit was planting seeds of vision in my soul.

Four months later, on January 8, 2012, I went back to Starbucks for
my regular meeting with Derek. I
showed up early to read my Bible
and pray. That morning, I read
Genesis 26, where God blessed
Isaac with a huge harvest, flocks,
and herds. Finally, Abimelech told
Isaac to leave. When he did, Isaac
settled in the valley of Gerar, and he
began to dig wells which had been
dug during the days of his father
Abraham. After a couple of attempts, God opened a space for Isaac.
God used the following words about Isaac to confirm, once again, His
plan for us to plant a church:

> **He went on from there
> and dug yet another well.
> But there was no fighting
> over this one so he named
> it Rehoboth (Wide-Open
> Spaces).**

*"He went on from there and dug yet another well. But there
was no fighting over this one so he named it Rehoboth (Wide-
Open Spaces), saying, "Now God has given us plenty of space to
spread out in the land." From there he went up to Beersheba.
That very night God appeared to him and said, I am the God of
Abraham your father; don't fear a thing because I'm with you.
I'll bless you and make your children flourish because of Abraham my servant. Isaac built an altar there and prayed, calling
on God by name. He pitched his tent and his servants started
digging another well" (Genesis 26:22-25, MSG).*

God was clearly calling us to dig a new well. God was calling us into
a wide-open space. Right after I read this passage, Derek arrived for
our meeting. In our conversation that morning, the subject of church
planting arose once again (I'm sure I started to sound like a broken

record). We discussed it for only a brief moment when suddenly, something changed. Derek began to speak to me with such authority and conviction that I knew in my spirit it was from the Lord. Looking back, I realize it was a prophetic, God-anointed word for my life. As soon as he finished speaking, I slid a napkin across the table and asked him to write down what God had just given him to say. On a Starbuck's napkin, he wrote these words:

> *"Don't be afraid to be out of the box, to throw the old box away and create something new. That is what the Lord does. He is creative, innovative in his very being. When you feel like I should do it this way or that way because this is how it is always done, don't be afraid to set that aside and do it your way. God is in the business of being fresh, new, creative. He delights in creativity. Be bold, be new, be fresh. Take risks and fail! God took a risk on man and knew it would fail and did it anyway. He knew [his] plan with Christ from the beginning. Be bold, be courageous, be creative!"* [63]

I suddenly felt an immense peace that God was with me and Karen in this journey—that He was calling us, and that He would lead us and take care of us.

Just a few days later, on January 14, 2012, while eating lunch at a local pizza restaurant, Karen and I made a decision to plant a church in the downtown or West 7th area of Fort Worth. I know, that sounds very random and obscure.

"Hey, let's eat some pizza. By the way, we should start a church."

"Sounds great! Wanna start tomorrow?"

Crazy, right?

I can assure you, they didn't spike the pizza.

Instead, years of praying and dreaming had finally come to a point of decision. I shared my conversations with Derek and Jeff and all the ways God had confirmed what I had sensed in my spirit over the past few months.

By this time, we had both finished our degrees, Ashley had graduated from high school, and I had peace from God that the timing was right. Over lunch that day, I told Karen that I really wanted to plant a church. Karen looked at me and said two simple words: "Me too."

There was a resolve in her voice. There was conviction, passion, and determination that planting a church was our next step. That was all I needed to hear. I felt like God had brought the final confirmation to His call.

Four days later I met with my pastor at Christ Church and shared our dream. In that conversation, Pastor Darius asked me, "Where do you want to plant?" I told him our heart was drawn to the downtown or West 7th area of Fort Worth. He told me about a small church that was struggling in that area, and he offered to talk to the pastor to see how things were going. I wasn't looking to move into an existing church, and I honestly thought we'd be renting space in a local movie theater or a conference center, but I was open to his suggestion.

After an initial conversation with the pastor of this small church, we discovered that the church was struggling, its building was in need of repairs, and it was facing a balloon payment at the end of that year. The congregation was approximately 25 people, and they were struggling to gain momentum. Plus, there was no parking, and they couldn't afford to rent the parking lot at the football stadium across the street. Combined with these difficult realities, the pastor was also sensing that his time at the church was coming to a close. He had done what he felt like the Lord had led him to do, part of which included moving the church to its current location.

Five months later, this small church closed, and we received a miracle. We inherited the building for what was owed on it: $109,000 (today it's valued at over $2 million). Plus, the 25 people in that church joined a group of people from Christ Church to form our launch team.

On May 27, 2012, we stood in front of the congregation as Pastor Darius boldly announced that we were going to plant a new church. From that day, we only had 16 weeks to come up with a name for the church, recruit a worship leader, build our teams, create our systems, develop our outreach plans, *and* renovate a building.

We worked 16 hours per day, for 16 weeks, and finally opened the doors of 7 City Church on September 16, 2012. It was an amazing day, and I was in awe of God's faithfulness through the entire process. It wasn't until eight months after we launched that I suddenly realized the significance of our launch date. On September 16, 2011, God moved on my heart to write down the vision for a new church. On September 16, 2012, *exactly one year later* (to the day), that vision became a reality.

Only God!

I am so humbled by what God did and what He has done. He is, and has always been, faithful. I recognize that our launch is not your typical church planting story. In fact, if you're a church planter, you probably feel like throwing rocks at me right now. Please know, I have the deepest respect for church planters, and I talk with planters on a regular basis, doing my best to offer help anyway I can. I'm quite aware, and quite humbled by the fact, that we were blessed with a strong launch team and a permanent facility. I'll always be thankful for what God did to make this happen.

> *God doesn't call us to the end of a diving board so that we can climb back down the ladder and return to Easy Street. He calls us into the unknown, a place that requires total trust in God.*

When you read this story, you might say, "Stephen, it would be easy to trust God with provision like that." I can understand why you might feel that way.

But I want to point out one important thing.

The provision didn't precede the "Yes."

Karen and I had to say yes to God before we ever knew about the provision God would bring our way. All of the prayers, wrestling, and confirmations brought us to a point of decision. We had to give God our answer. We were standing on the edge of the diving board, and we had to choose whether or not we would jump.

We chose to jump.

Before we knew about the building.

Before we knew about the miracles God would do.

Before we ever talked to Pastor Darius.

God wanted to know, "Are you in, or are you out?"

We chose to go "all in."

It is very easy to depend on ourselves. It is very easy to pretend the Lord hasn't spoken, and to do things our own way. But God doesn't call us to the end of a diving board so that we can climb back down the ladder and return to Easy Street. He calls us into the unknown, a place that requires total trust in God.

While God has done miracles, we have also faced plenty of resistance. Heart and pulmonary failure, physical hardships, attacks from people, unexpected setbacks, staff transitions, leading during a pandemic, and many more roadblocks that required steps of faith. But we know God spoke to us to start 7 City Church. That *knowledge* has sustained us during the most difficult days. It has given us the confidence that God is with us, and He can be trusted.

Where's Your Confidence?

How do you jump off the diving board when so much fear and uncertainty fill your mind? It begins with a God-inspired confidence. All of us place our confidence in somewhere, someone, or something. Confidence can be either a firm source of peace about the future or it can be an unstable footing that keeps us living in panic. The apostle Paul placed his confidence in the firm foundation of the Lord. Paul said:

> *"If the Lord Jesus is willing, I hope to send Timothy to you soon for a visit. Then he can cheer me up by telling me how you are getting along. I have no one else like Timothy, who genuinely cares about your welfare. All the others care only for themselves and not for what matters to Jesus Christ. But you know how Timothy has proved himself. Like a son with his father, he has served with me in preaching the Good News. I hope to send him to you just as soon as I find out what is going to happen to me here. And* I have confidence from the Lord *that I myself will come to see you soon" (Philippians 2:19-24, emphasis added).*

Paul's future was uncertain; would he face years in prison or death? Paul couldn't trust his precarious circumstances, so he placed his confidence in his unshakeable God. God had delivered him before, and Paul was certain He would do it again. Prison walls couldn't confine his faith. The officials who stole his freedom couldn't rob his trust in God.

When you stop chasing easy, you'll be tempted to place your confidence in the things you see with your natural eyes. Instead, anchor your confidence in Christ. Trust in the One who climbs the ladder of vision beside you, walks to the edge of the diving board behind you, and awaits your arrival in the pool in front of you. That's when your faith grows, your character matures, and you make your life count today—and for eternity.

Chapter 10
Honor
Express Character by Elevating Others

Most of us are quite fond of the attention we receive when we're honored by others. Let's be honest, it can be music to our ears when friends, family, or coworkers sing our praises or tout our successes. It's encouraging and uplifting when people notice how hard we've worked and how faithfully we've served. A simple word of affirmation, acknowledgement of our effort, or heartfelt expression of appreciation can go a long way to make us feel loved and valued. Honor is a good thing, and it can pull out the very best in people.

Unfortunately, some people have abused the idea of honor. They've used it as a means to manipulate or a tactic to intimidate. Some have demanded honor to get what they want, or they've guilted people into honor by shaming them at the slightest hint of disagreement. Some have even been spiritually abusive in the name of "honor."

So, what does healthy honor look like? Healthy honor isn't about controlling or demeaning others. Instead, it's about expressing our belief in people and celebrating others. It's looking for the good in people and then giving voice to their value. True honor is the deliberate choice to use our words

> *True honor is the deliberate choice to use our words and behavior to show respect, esteem, and regard for others without feeling threatened by their success.*

and behavior to show respect, esteem, and regard for others without feeling threatened by their success. It's a willingness to recognize those who have travelled before us, beside us, or after us, and to honor their gifts, sacrifice, and faithfulness. Healthy honor is a two-way street. It's delivered up and down, and side to side, and it's expressed through our attitudes and actions.

Honor in Action

One of the most honorable people I know is Darius Johnston. I served on Pastor Darius' staff for several years, and I still consider him my pastor today. He exhibits the most gracious, kind, and loving attitude, and he truly knows how to honor people in the most meaningful ways.

When I see Pastor Darius talking with kids or students, he is always full of joy, positivity, and a contagious cheerfulness. When I see him interacting with the elderly, he is quick to show them respect for the path they've blazed before him. And when he talks with people who are broken, hurting, and defeated, he shows the most extraordinary grace. To each person, his honor expresses belief, appreciation, and compassion. Even if he disagrees with you, he does so in a way that makes you feel respected and valued. After one conversation with Pastor Darius, you leave hopeful and encouraged. It's who he is. It's part of his character.

One of the most meaningful times in which I encountered Pastor Darius' honoring spirit was when Karen and I planted 7 City Church. Many pastors feel threatened by other churches, especially churches that are located nearby. Other pastors get territorial when a new church siphons off a few sheep for their congregation. Not Pastor Darius. He leads with an open hand and a humble heart.

No pastor wants to lose people. But for years, I've watched Pastor Darius refuse to be fearful when another church flourishes. Rather than giving jealousy room in his heart, he cheers others on, recognizing that we're all on the same team.

In the last chapter, I told you about our journey of planting 7 City Church. Pastor Darius played an extraordinarily significant role in that entire process. We would not be where we are today without his willingness to believe in us. We would not have started with a strong launch team, or secured a facility in a great location, without his guidance, help, and support. But what I didn't tell you in the last chapter is what happened just four months prior to sharing our church planting dream with him.

Four months earlier—in September 2011—Pastor Darius sent another staff member, along with a team of several dozen people, and tens of thousands of dollars, to plant a church west of Fort Worth. Most pastors would have taken a couple of years (or longer) to recover before sending out *another* staff member to plant *another* church. Most pastors would have told me, "No way, not now. It's too quick, too soon, too risky."

But, despite the recent departure of a church planting team, Pastor Darius still said "Yes!" Even when I offered to wait 18-24 months before leaving to start 7 City Church, his first question was, "Where do you want to plant?" He refused to let his vision for new, healthy churches be inhibited by fear. He has honored the dreams of countless pastors, churches, and missionaries, and I've seen God honor him time and again for his Kingdom-minded leadership. Each time he opens his hand, God has faithfully provided.[64]

Paul on Honor

I'm not sure where Pastor Darius learned to be so honoring, but he might have taken a cue from the apostle Paul. Constrained by chains, Paul could have easily dismissed the importance of honor. He could have let the fear of being forgotten—or the fear of losing influence— steal his honoring spirit. He could have sunk into despair, convinced his days were done, while others advanced the Gospel without his help. Instead, Paul honored others and refused to let jealousy get the best of him. In his letter to the Philippians, he wrote:

> *"Meanwhile, I thought I should send Epaphroditus back to you. He is a true brother, co-worker, and fellow soldier. And he was your messenger to help me in my need.* I am sending him because he has been longing to see you, *and he was very distressed that you heard he was ill. And he certainly was ill; in fact, he almost died. But God had mercy on him—and also on me, so that I would not have one sorrow after another. So* I am all the more anxious to send him back to you, *for I know you will be glad to see him, and then I will not be so worried about you.* Welcome him in the Lord's love and with great joy, and give him the honor that people like him deserve. *For he*

risked his life for the work of Christ, and he was at the point of
death while doing for me what you couldn't do from far away"
(Philippians 2:25-30, NLT, emphasis added).

Something strikes me about Paul's spirit of honor in this passage. Honoring wasn't just an attitude; it was an everyday action. It was part of his character. And from Paul's example, we discover three practical ways to express honor to others.

1. Honor by Empowering with Opportunity

Paul could have easily kept Epaphroditus by his side. He could have created a case as to why Epaphroditus should stick with Paul during Paul's time of need. Instead, Paul released him. He empowered Epaphroditus by sending him to the Philippian believers. He even said, "I am all the more anxious to send him back to you." Paul didn't send Epaphroditus because he had to, he sent him because it was time to share Epaphroditus's gifts.

Too often we like to hold on to people, even when it's time for them to go. We see this all the time when parents can't (or won't) let their kids leave the nest and pursue their dreams. We see it in leadership circles when leaders hold staff members with a closed fist, afraid to lose the gifts, abilities, and skills they bring to the organization.

Good parents recognize that their job is not to raise co-dependent kids, but rather healthy adults. And good leaders recognize that they do not *own* people. Instead, they've been entrusted with people for a season, and when that season comes to an end, their job is to empower those they lead for their next season.

When Karen and I started 7 City Church, one of the commitments we made personally was to always hold people with an open hand. God brought them to us, and God could take them away—*as* He chooses and *when* He chooses. That's not always easy, especially when somebody close to you leaves—somebody who has served the vision faithfully or played an important role in the journey.

We've seen staff, leaders, friends, and volunteers leave. But God did not call us to hold people tightly; he called us to honor them freely. When a core volunteer comes to you and says, "I feel like God is leading us to another church," you choose to support them. When a staff member says, "I feel like God is calling me to a new opportunity," you congratulate them and then ask, "How can I support you in the process?" We haven't done this perfectly, but we try to see these moments as a way for the Kingdom of God to expand.

Remember, they're not *your* people. They're God's people, and He can choose to move them when and how He wants (without asking for your permission). Rather than letting your insecurities get the best of you, honor the people you value through their transition.

I learned this from Pastor Darius. Even if it was a volunteer who left the church, he would always say, "You want to be able to see this person in the grocery store and not feel like you have to walk down the other aisle." He knew how to honor others in difficult moments to prevent unnecessary awkwardness.

That was a powerful lesson, and it helped me understand both the immediate and long-term value of honoring others.

> **Rather than letting your insecurities get the best of you, honor the people you value through their transition.**

Honoring through empowerment also shows up in moments of faithful service. In the parable of the talents (Matthew 25), most of us focus on the faithfulness of the servants (which is certainly important). After all, the master told two of his servants, "Well done, my good and faithful servant. You have been faithful in handling this small amount, so now I will give you many more responsibilities. Let's celebrate together!" (Matthew 25:23). But there's another lesson in this parable that is often overlooked—*how to treat a faithful person*. When you look at the master, you discover that he did three things for his faithful servants:

- He *commended them* for their faithful service.
- He *entrusted them* with greater opportunity.
- He *rewarded them* by celebrating together.[65]

Simply put, the master honored his servants with three-dimensional empowerment: the words he spoke, the opportunities he delegated, and the celebrations he hosted.

2. Honor by Acknowledging Hopes and Dreams

The second way Paul expressed a spirit of honor was by acknowledging Epaphroditus' desire to see the Philippians. Paul said, "he has been longing to see you." Honorable people take a genuine interest in the hopes and dreams of those around them. Sometimes those hopes and dreams are personal, while other times they're professional.

When a friend or family member shares with you a personal dream, how do you respond? Do you acknowledge the dream and then cheer them on? Do you express how much you believe in them? Do you offer to help any way you can? Or do you critique, criticize, and crush their dreams? One of the best ways you can show honor is by being a cheerleader for the hopes, dreams, and aspirations of others.

I try to practice this with our team at 7 City. Each year during staff reviews, not only do I give important feedback on their performance, but I also use this time to inquire about their future hopes and dreams. For example, I'll ask each team member questions like, "How are you feeling about your role?" and "What would you do, or what would you attempt for God, if you knew you could not fail?" By asking these questions on a self-assessment prior to our meeting, they have time to think about their answers. Once I hear their responses, I acknowledge what they're sensing, and then look for ways to honor their aspirations. Sometimes those dreams can be fulfilled at 7 City Church. Other times they choose to pursue new opportunities in other places.

3. Honor by Recognizing Faithfulness

Finally, cultivate a spirit of honor by recognizing the faithfulness of others. Paul told the Philippians, "Welcome him in the Lord's love and with great joy, and give him the honor that people like him deserve" (Philippians 2:29). Epaphroditus had worked hard—even risking his life for the Gospel—and Paul wanted him to be welcomed with open arms and honored for his faithful service.

Easy Street is consumed with self-promotion, but the road that counts recognizes that other people deserve honor and support.

I have to remind myself to acknowledge faithfulness regularly. It's easy to get tunnel vision when you focus on the task at hand, the never-ending list of responsibilities, and the ever-increasing pressures of leadership. If we're not careful, we'll forget to stop and say thank you, celebrate wins, and show honor where honor is due. People work hard, and they should be appreciated for their faithful service.

Easy Street is consumed with self-promotion, but the road that counts recognizes that other people deserve honor and support. We can't be threatened by someone else's success. Instead, we should honor others by modeling character mature enough to offer recognition and affirmation to the people around us.

Cultivating "Stop Chasing Easy" Maturity

In the last five chapters, we've discovered the kind of character that helps us stop chasing easy. We've learned the importance of MATU-RITY, and the role it plays as we trade short-sighted pursuits for a life that counts for eternity. This maturity is seen in the development of five character traits that will enable us to withstand the pressures outside of Easy Street. Without character we'll self-destruct, regardless of any noble mission. But if you'll focus on your *who* (your character), God will give you strength for your *what* (your mission). Trading comfort for character isn't easy, but you can begin with love, humble service, obedience, trust, and honor.

Part 3: Mission
Trade Temporal for Eternal

If we're going to stop chasing easy, we begin with the right MIND-SET—trading pessimism for perspective. As you recall, there are five mindsets essential to stop chasing easy and pursue a life that counts: thankfulness, growth, opportunity, big picture, and perseverance. Each of these perspectives gives you the mental strength to not only leave Easy Street, but to stay focused on what matters most.

In addition to the right MINDSET, we must commit to MATURITY and trade comfort for character. If your character is weak, shallow, or undeveloped, you'll be crushed under the weight of whatever God calls you to do. As we learned in the last few chapters, there are five character qualities to build maturity: love, humble service, obedience, trust, and honor. Growing each of these character traits is not a once and done activity. But if you commit to their ongoing development, you'll grow into the person God has called you to become and establish the inner strength to carry the weight of your God-given mission. This is where we turn our attention now: MISSION—trading the temporal for the eternal.

Our culture is drunk on pursuit. The pursuit of happiness and health, riches and relationships. The pursuit of fame, power, sex, and success. We take giant gulps of pleasure, trying to satisfy our thirst for more. We drink in intoxicating lies, thinking we'll discover meaning and purpose. We swallow the promises of gain and gratification, only to find those promises broken time and again.

The lies leave us empty.

The broken promises reveal our own failings.

Each of these pursuits are temporal. We long for a peace and a purpose that is permanent, but our chase only leads us to the dead-end of Easy Street. Easy Street is littered with lives built on temporal success rather than eternal significance.

And that brings us to the third trade-off.

If you want exchange Easy Street for the pursuit of a life that counts, you must trade *temporal* for *eternal*.

Over the next five chapters, we'll dive-in to Philippians chapter three. In these 21 verses, Paul gives us five keys that make the trade-off from temporal to eternal possible.

First, we'll discover the temporal nature of success, and how to keep it from luring us back to Easy Street. Success isn't bad. In fact, God often gives us success. But a mission focused on success alone is empty, which is why we'll also learn how to embrace an eternal mission. Once we discover significance, we'll learn how to focus on it each day and how to seek out mentors so our mission becomes a reality. Finally, we'll be reminded of our eternal home—heaven. It will keep us grounded in who we are and what matters most.

The trade-off from temporal to eternal is a major step outside of Easy Street. It's where we identify a new destination—a compelling MISSION—so we can make a difference in our slice of the world. This doesn't mean that you become so heavenly-minded that you have no earthly value. Instead, your priorities and affections become so eternally focused that you do the greatest earthly good possible. Simply put, what you do matters beyond today and into the future for ten million tomorrows and beyond.

Let's make the trade-off: rather than dancing on the streets of self-serving pleasure and short-sighted priorities, trade the temporal for the eternal and pursue a mission that matters.

Chapter 11

Success

See Beyond the Temporal

A t the start of every new year, millions of people resolve to start something new. You've probably tried this a time or two yourself (it might even be a yearly ritual for you). Your resolution might be to start exercising. Maybe you're determined to turn the start of a new year into the start of a new career. Perhaps your plan is to return to school, launch a new business, or pick up a new hobby. Every year starts with *starting*.

But we also like to quit.

Our "Quit List" is often longer than our "Start List." In fact, a few days into the beginning of one year I did a Google search on quitting and discovered you can learn to quit all kinds of things: smoking, drinking, biting your nails, dipping, weed, bad habits, Weight Watchers, caffeine, energy drinks, fast food, gambling, whining, junk food, Diet Coke…the quitting options were endless. You could even learn how to quit quitting.

Why are *starting* and *quitting* so popular when a new year rolls off the press, its blank pages waiting for fresh headlines? Because we want tomorrow to look different. Our dissatisfaction with our current reality thrusts us into a search for success. The problem most people don't realize is that our definition of success is often skewed. As author Stephen Covey said, "If the ladder is not leaning against the right wall, every step we take just gets us to the wrong place faster."[66]

Maybe you can relate.

Or maybe you feel like you're at a fork in the road, unsure which path will lead you to your desired destination. In Lewis Carroll's classic, *Alice in Wonderland*, Alice searched for a way out of Wonderland. When she came to a fork in the road, she asked the Cheshire Cat, "Which road should I take?" The Cat replied, "Where are you going?" Alice didn't have an answer, so the Cheshire Cat simply said, "If you don't know where you're going, any road can take you there."[67] It's cute in a work of fiction, but not so funny in real life.

> *If you're climbing a ladder that's leaning against the wrong building, what does it matter? Who cares about success if its focus is only temporal?*

Chasing success is thrilling, adventurous, even addicting and can even produce amazing results when it comes to money, power, opportunity, and influence. The problem is, these are temporary measures of success. They only focus on today. Without a greater purpose, these results leave you feeling empty as they drive you down a dead-end street.

Success cannot grow on Easy Street. In fact, success is hard work, and money, power, and influence are the paychecks you receive when you put in the long hours and endless energy to achieve your dreams. But again, if you're climbing a ladder that's leaning against the wrong building, what does it matter? Who cares about success if its focus is *only* temporal?

I'm not suggesting that success is wrong or that the blessings that often come with success are inherently evil. In fact, I've seen God bless many people with wonderful success in their endeavors, whether at home, at school, or in their careers. I'm simply saying that success alone is not enough. The real purpose of success is to set us up for significance (but I'm getting ahead of myself).

Paul's Climb to Temporary Success

As Philippians chapter three unfolds, we get a very sobering glimpse of Paul's rapid ascent up the ladder of success, only to discover it was leaning against a temporary structure. He sets the stage with these words:

> *Whatever happens, my dear brothers and sisters, rejoice in the*

Lord. I never get tired of telling you these things, and I do it to safeguard your faith. Watch out for those dogs, those people who do evil, those mutilators who say you must be circumcised to be saved. For we who worship by the Spirit of God are the ones who are truly circumcised. We rely on what Christ Jesus has done for us. We put no confidence in human effort, though I could have confidence in my own effort if anyone could. Indeed, if others have reason for confidence in their own efforts, I have even more! (Philippians 3:1-4)

Why did Paul have so much confidence in human effort? What successes gave him so much credibility? Paul had impressive credentials before he ever became a follower of Jesus. He was an elite religious leader of his day, and his accomplishments put him in the upper stratosphere of his career. In fact, as we continue reading this passage, we discover three of the rungs in Paul's ladder of success.

1. Heritage

Paul said, "I was circumcised when I was eight days old. I am a pure-blooded citizen of Israel and a member of the tribe of Benjamin" (Philippians 3:5a). First, like all good male Jews, Paul was circumcised. This was a non-negotiable rite to Judaism. Second, Paul didn't have to convert to Judaism because he was a pure-blooded citizen of Israel. In other words, he was born into God's people. Third, Paul was from the tribe of Benjamin, one of the most respected tribes in Israel. In fact, Paul came from a family of pure Benjamites who didn't intermarry with other tribes.[68] Simply put, Paul was successful by virtue of where he came from. He was born into the right family, and with that heritage came certain privileges.

2. Achievements

Paul continues the description of his climb to success when he writes, "a real Hebrew if there ever was one! I was a member of the Pharisees, who demand the strictest obedience to the Jewish law. I was so zealous that I harshly persecuted the church" (Philippians 3:5b-6a). As a "real Hebrew," Paul maintained his family heritage—including the language, traditions, and customs—right into adulthood. On top of that, he studied under a famous Rabi named Gamaliel. Paul was also a Pharisee. When you and I think of Pharisees today, we think of people who are hypocritical, judgmental, and fail to practice what they preach. But in Paul's day, Pharisees were viewed in a positive light and with a great deal of respect. They were considered the elite of the religious elite.

Pastor and author Larry Osborne observed, "In Jesus's day, being called a Pharisee was a badge of honor. It was a compliment, not a slam. That's because first-century Pharisees excelled in everything we admire spiritually. They were zealous for God, completely committed to their faith. They were theologically astute, masters of the biblical texts. They fastidiously obeyed even the most obscure commands. They even made up extra rules just in case they were missing anything. Their embrace of spiritual disciplines was second to none."[69] To be a Pharisee put you at the top of the religious order of the day.

Paul's achievements didn't stop there—he zealously and harshly persecuted the church. In Paul's day, zeal was considered a religious virtue that involved both love and hate. It meant a deep love for God and a deep hate for anything that was opposed to God. Before Paul encountered Jesus, he viewed himself as being so zealous in his love for God that he hated Christians, and therefore he persecuted them. In his mind, he was doing what was right.[70]

3. Reputation

The pinnacle of Paul's climb to success is seen in his statement, "as for righteousness, I obeyed the law without fault" (Philippians 3:6b). Basically, Paul was the perfect model of a devoted Jew. You could say that Paul was the CEO of religious success. He was at the top of his game and his reputation was spotless.

Moving Beyond a Temporary Mission

Each one of us has our own definition of success. It might not be written out on a piece of paper, but inside our heads we keep a measure that we use to define whether we're winning or losing. For some of us, it's tied to our heritage. Maybe you were born into a family that afforded you financial privileges or doors of opportunity that most people don't have. On the other hand, maybe your heritage is full of blemishes and brokenness. We may measure ourselves against our heritage, but, as we'll see in a moment, Paul uses some strong words to express how he really feels about his heritage.

Maybe for you, success isn't about your heritage but rather your achievements and your reputation. Perhaps you've achieved a desirable level of success marked by a great college degree, a flourishing business, a recent promotion, or name recognition. You've worked hard, and you've got the resume to prove it. You've built a solid reputation, and others look to you as the expert in your field. Or, maybe you're on the opposite end of the spectrum. Maybe your reputation is riddled with failures, disappointments, and regrets. Again, hang on, because Paul's about to tell us what he really thinks of his own achievements and reputation.

After Paul's radical encounter with Jesus on the road to Damascus (Acts 9), his life was completely transformed. With that transformation, Paul began to look at his success differently. He even said of a legalistic group of Jews called the Judaizers, "The very credentials these people are waving around as something special, I'm tearing up and throwing out with the trash—along with everything else I used to take credit for" (Philippians 3:7-8a, MSG). If Paul had no credentials of his own, I could understand why he would react this way. But that wasn't the case. Everybody's credentials paled in comparison to Paul's. But when Jesus intersects your life and turns everything upside down, your priorities get reorganized. Suddenly, life is not just about today; the eternal becomes more important than the temporal.

> **When you look at your success, has it become an end in itself? If so, maybe it's time to climb a new ladder, one that leans against eternal values and an eternal mission.**

Here's my question for you: When you look at your success, has it become an end in itself? If so, maybe it's time to climb a new ladder, one that leans against eternal values and an eternal mission.

Again, please hear me correctly. I'm not suggesting that your heritage, achievements, or reputation are worthless. Heritage can be a blessing. Your achievements and reputation can be signs of solid character and hard work. But what would happen if these resources were placed in God's hands to be used for His glory? Success was never meant to be an end in itself. Instead, it was meant to be a catalyst for a greater mission. The last thing God wants is for any of us to wake up at the end of life wondering why our pursuit of a temporal mission left us empty. Today matters...and so does eternity.

Reframing Success

Several years ago, I sat in a leadership conference and heard Phil Vischer share an extraordinary story of success, a humbling crash into failure, and a lifegiving message of hope. At the age of 25, in an effort to integrate his faith with filmmaking, Phil created the popular kids video series called, "VeggieTales," featuring Bob the Tomato, Larry the Cucumber, and several other talking vegetables who taught kids valuable lessons based on biblical principles.

This innovative series sold more than 65 million copies, but at the peak of Phil's success, everything took a nosedive. "Over-aggressive expansion coupled with a lawsuit from a former distributor forced Phil's company, Big Idea Productions, into bankruptcy in 2003."[71] After fourteen years of back-breaking work, Phil lost it all—his company, his characters, and his dream.

How did it happen? Not the lawsuit. Not the bankruptcy. What were the early steps that led to this downward spiral? Reflecting back on his crash, Phil said, "Rather than finding my identity in my relationship with God, I was finding it in my drive to do 'good work.' The more I dove into Scripture, the more I realized that I had been deluded. I had grown up drinking a dangerous cocktail—a mix of the gospel, the Protestant work ethic, and the American dream."[72]

Wow! How easy it is to let accolades and accomplishments dupe us into believing that achievement and success is the pinnacle of life. Phil had a great product (one that even taught eternal values), but he was being blinded by temporal measures of success.

Phil goes on to explain that as he navigated this painful journey, he heard a sermon that transformed his perspective. The person preaching said, "If God gives you a dream, and the dream comes to life and God shows up in it, and then the dream dies, it may be that God wants to see what is more important to you—the dream or him."[73]

Today, Phil Vischer lives with a different perspective. He reframed success. Rather than defining his success by the temporal values of Phil's own kingdom, he has tapped into the eternal perspective of a greater Kingdom. Phil is still writing, making films, and helping families, but now he's doing it with a different motive and a new definition of success.

What about you? Do you need to reframe or redefine success? Do you need to shift from a temporal view to an eternal view, and then live today with motives and ambitions that honor the Lord? In the next chapter, I'll show you how to make the shift, and what it looks like to pursue a mission with eternal value.

Chapter 12
Significance
Embrace Your Eternal Mission

As a 12-year old boy, Hal Donaldson's world was turned upside down after hearing a knock at the door. It was 7:35 pm on August 25, 1969, and Hal, along with his two younger brothers, his five-year old sister, and their babysitter, opened the door to find two police officers. They had come to deliver devastating news that would rock the children's world; their mom and dad had been involved in a head-on collision with a drunk driver. Their dad—only 37 years old—was dead, and their mom was fighting for her life.[74]

Neighbors were gathering when one of the police officers said, "Are there any family members or friends here who will take responsibility for the children tonight. Otherwise, we'll take them downtown to the station." A young couple named Bill and Louvada Davis stepped forward and volunteered. That one-night sleepover stretched much longer.[75]

For many months, while their mom was recovering in the hospital, the kids slept with the Davis family in a single-wide trailer. Bill and Louvada drained their savings so four kids could have a place to live while their mom slowly regained her health and learned to walk again. After her recovery, Hal's mom got a job as a mail clerk, and the family moved into their own place.

But life would be different.

Poverty became their new reality.

When bitterness would try to put down roots in Hal's heart, Bill

Davis would tell him, "Don't allow the tragedy of your childhood to become a lifelong excuse, because where you start in life doesn't have to dictate where you end."[76]

Hal eventually graduated high school, then college, and then entered the workforce as a journalist. He was determined to leave his disadvantaged childhood behind. Though he never forgot the lessons he learned from Bill and Louvada, Hal quickly became consumed with his success as a journalist. His travels took him around the world, and in his busyness, he would say, "Someday, I'll give back and help the less fortunate, but my career has to come first."[77]

> **Our success rarely has a deadline, and our appetite for success is never fully satisfied. It usually takes something bold or unforgettable to jar us out of our shortsighted ambition.**

It's easy to convince ourselves that our success matters most. After all, if I'm successful, my needs will be met. If I achieve greatness, I can help others become great, too. But our success rarely has a deadline, and our appetite for success is never fully satisfied. It usually takes something bold or unforgettable to jar us out of our shortsighted ambition. That's what happened to Hal.

His global journalism travels took him to India, where he met Mother Teresa. During a brief 20-minute interview, Hal scribbled her quotes as fast as he could in his notebook. But then time stood still when Mother Teresa asked Hal a question that would haunt him: "Young man, can I ask what you do to help the poor?"

Hal said, "I'm really not doing anything."

Mother Teresa didn't condemn or chastise him. Instead, she gently said, "Everyone can do something."[78]

On that same trip, after seeing so much crippling poverty, Hal asked Missionary Mark Buntain how he and his wife Huldah kept from getting overwhelmed. Mark simply replied, "We stay focused on what we can do—not what we can't. We were never asked to play god—that's his job. We can't do everything, but that can't be an excuse for doing nothing."[79] Those encounters with Mother Teresa and Mark and Huldah Buntain set Hal on a search for significance. He longed for a purpose and a mission that would outlast him.

One day, in 1994, Hal made a decision that would bring his mission to life. Along with his two brothers, Hal began loading pickup trucks and U-Haul trailers with groceries and supplies to give to poor working families in California. Mother Teresa's words, "Everyone can do something," took root in Hal's heart and began producing fruit through his efforts. Hal said, "With each passing day, selfishness became more distasteful and selflessness more satisfying."[80] Those early acts of compassion didn't stop. They were the seeds that grew into a global humanitarian relief organization that today we know as Convoy of Hope.

Since those early days, Convoy has served over 115 million people. They provide disaster relief around the world. If you see a news report about a hurricane, tsunami, earthquake, flood, or wildfire, you can almost bet Convoy of Hope is on the scene distributing clean water, providing meals, and offering support in the middle of the devastation.

Convoy also feeds well over 300,000 children through their food programs, and they equip vulnerable farmers with training and resources to produce stronger crops. Additionally, they empower women around the world with training and education to start their own businesses. And when Covid-19 devastated lives and left families jobless, Convoy distributed more than 200 million meals.[81]

> Hal: "With each passing day, selfishness became more distasteful and selflessness more satisfying."

Hal is living a life of significance, but it wasn't—and isn't—easy. Significance is never found on Easy Street. It's only found when we redefine success, and it's only experienced when we embrace a mission that matters—not just for today, but for eternity.

How to Find Your Eternal Mission

Maybe you read Hal Donaldson's story and said, "Stephen, that's amazing, but I could never do that. I don't have the gifting, resources, connections, or even the desire." That's fine. Besides, that's what God has called Hal to do. The real question is, what has God called *you* to do? Just because you don't start a global organization like Convoy of Hope doesn't mean you're off the hook for making a difference. God has still called you to steer clear of Easy Street and embrace an eternal mission.

So, what determines if a mission has "eternal" significance? It's *outward*, *upward*, and *inward*. In other words, a mission has eternal significance when it serves someone beside you (outward), when it's aligned with the values of God's Kingdom (upward), and when your internal motives for pursuing it are pure (inward). So, how do you discover that kind of mission—one that adds value today and matters for eternity? Let's start with the outward focus of serving others. It begins by asking five core questions.

1. What gifts do I have?

You're going to make your greatest contribution to your slice of the world through your God-given gifts. God will never ask you to use someone else's gifts to accomplish your life mission, but He will hold you accountable to wisely steward the resources He has entrusted to you. Your unique gifts include spiritual gifts, natural abilities, acquired skills, influence, knowledge, and financial resources. That unique gift mix will help you answer the next four questions.

2. What need can I meet?

Look around you. Every part of your community is plagued with needs. There are spiritual needs, relational needs, financial needs, and emotional needs. People are hungry, lonely, depressed, homeless, suicidal, or jobless. There are kids in need of tutoring, single moms in need of childcare, widows in need of compassion, coworkers in need of a listening ear, and non-profits in need of leaders, volunteers, and financial support. How can you use your gifts, abilities, skills, influence, knowledge, and resources to meet a need that taps into your passion?

3. What problem can I solve?

Problems tend to be larger than needs. For example, you might meet a need by feeding a hungry family, but you haven't solved their problem. In a few hours, they'll be hungry again. That doesn't mean that meeting their need isn't important. In fact, it's critical, especially during crises and emergencies. But maybe God has called you to take another step and help solve a problem for a person, a group, an organization, or even an entire community. It might be a spiritual problem, an educational problem, a healthcare problem, a work-related problem, or a problem unique to your neighborhood, church, or community. Again, your gifts, abilities, skills, influence, knowledge, and resources are the

God-given tools you can use to solve that problem.

4. What person can I help?

Jesus called us to love our neighbors, and one of the greatest ways to love our neighbor is by simply helping them. Your neighbor might literally be a next-door neighbor or, they might be a classmate, a colleague, a homeless person, or the parents of a child on your daughter's soccer team. Who needs your help, and what can you do to help them today? Maybe they need you to mow their lawn while they deal with an unexpected medical emergency. Maybe they could use some help carpooling the kids to school. Or maybe you need to share the good news of Jesus with them.

5. What beauty can I create?

Our culture is in desperate need of God-honoring expressions of beauty. Whether it's through painting, drawing, photography, video, music, design, decorating, or some other form of art, what can you do to make your part of the world flourish with a bit more beauty. Once again, your God-given gifts are your toolkit to make your part of the world shine.

These are five simple questions, but don't underestimate their ability to jolt you out of easy and into a life of significance. And if you think these questions have nothing to do with eternity, then let me remind you of the eternal, Kingdom values Jesus continually emphasized: values like love, servanthood, and doing unto others as you would have them do unto you. His entire mission was oriented around others.

Not only that, but our daily activity is connected to eternity. In other words, what you do today matters tomorrow. In Colossians 3:23-24, Paul said, "Work willingly at whatever you do, as though you were working for the Lord rather than for people. Remember that the Lord will give you an inheritance as your reward, and that the Master you are serving is Christ." Your service to others matters to God, because in serving others you serve the Lord himself. Whether in the community, at church, through a cause, on a campus, or in your career, what you do and how you do it matters (today and forever). Author and pastor Andy Stanley observed, "Your work has eternal implications

Andy Stanley: "Your work has eternal implications even if it has no apparent eternal value."

even if it has no apparent eternal value."[82]

Again, an eternal mission begins with an *outward* focus. That's one thing that separates success from significance. So much success is self-centered, but significance looks beyond personal gain and invests in serving others. If you really want the success God has given to you to count eternally, then leverage it to meet needs, solve problems, help people, and create beauty.

Living in the Significance Sweet Spot

When you discover your mission by answering the five questions above, you'll reorient your life *outwardly*. The next step is to align your life *upwardly* (with eternal values) and *inwardly* (with pure motives). This happens when you start living in the "significance sweet spot." Think of the significance sweet spot as the place where three circles overlap on a Venn diagram. Those three circles are your *relationship with God*, the *power of God*, and *sacrifice for God*. This was Paul's approach to living with eternity in mind.

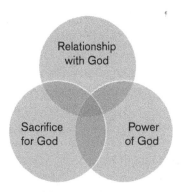

1. A relationship with God

Paul said, "Everything else is worthless when compared with the infinite value of *knowing Christ Jesus* my Lord" (Philippians 3:8a, emphasis added). He fully let go of his former definition of success and replaced it with the most significant pursuit possible: knowing Christ. He came to the realization that eternal significance is only possible when framed in a relationship with the eternal Son of God.

You will not be completely fulfilled outside of a relationship with Jesus. Your heritage, achievements, and reputation will not satisfy the deepest yearning of your heart. That's why Paul said, "For his sake I have discarded everything else, counting it all as garbage, so that I could gain Christ and become one with him. I no longer count on my own righteousness through obeying the law; rather, I become righteous through faith in Christ. For God's way of making us right with himself depends on faith" (Philippians 3:8b-9).

For Paul, knowing Christ was an ongoing relationship that shaped, formed, and transformed him into the man he became. It changed his values (upward), and it purified his motives (inward). Without a relationship with God, your interior life will collapse under the weight of your mission. Even worse, your heart will be hijacked by the idols of success, approval, and platform-building.

So, where does a relationship with Christ begin? In his letter to the Romans, Paul said, "So we

When we place our faith in Christ, we are made right with God, and our lives are aligned upwardly and inwardly with Jesus.

are made right with God through faith and not by obeying the law" (Romans 3:28). Everything Paul did before coming to Christ was focused on his obedience to the law. But the law does not save us. It only points us to our need for a Savior. Law reminds us of our sin, and it tells us we're not good enough to perfectly obey it.

We need a Savior.

We need forgiveness.

We need grace.

Paul came to realize that Jesus alone is that Savior, and at the end of the day, knowing Him is what matters most. When we place our faith in Christ, we are made right with God, and our lives are aligned upwardly and inwardly with Jesus.

2. The Power of God

Paul didn't stop at knowing Christ. In Philippians 3:10, he said, "I want to know Christ and experience the mighty power that raised him from the dead." The resurrection power of Jesus begins when we place our faith in Christ and become spiritually alive, but Christ's power doesn't end there. In Christ we have:

- Power in our weakness (2 Corinthians 12:9)
- Power to do all things (Philippians 4:13)

- Power to proclaim the Gospel (1 Corinthians 2:4)
- Power to live in a godly manner (2 Peter 1:3)
- Power over fear (2 Timothy 1:7)
- Power in our weariness (Isaiah 40:29)
- Power to be His witness (Acts 1:8)

The Gospel isn't powerless, and Paul understood that its power changes everything. He longed to experience ever-increasing measures of Christ's resurrection power. His power enables us to pursue a mission beyond our own strength (and beyond today), and to do so with motives that honor the Lord.

3. Sacrifice for God

Not only did Paul want to know Christ and experience His resurrection power, but he said, "I want to suffer with him, sharing in his death, so that one way or another I will experience the resurrection from the dead!" (Philippians 3:10b-11). Paul identified with Christ's power, but he also identified with Christ's death. Through Jesus' death, the power of sin was put to death, and as a follower of Jesus, Paul was committed to dying daily to the passions of his sin nature.[83] Simply put, Paul was willing to make whatever sacrifices were necessary to live for Christ and to share Christ with others. As I heard my friend Scott Wilson once say, "Sacrifice is giving up something of value to you so something of greater value can be accomplished in and through you for the Kingdom of God." Pursuing an eternal mission always requires sacrifice today.

Bringing it All Together

When we answer the five questions, and then choose to live each day in the significance sweet spot, our lives become focused outwardly and aligned upwardly and inwardly. This is when we begin making our greatest impact both today and for eternity. Think of it like the merging of a *place* and a *posture*. In other words, the five questions help you determine the *place* where you can serve. The significance sweet spot helps you develop the *posture* to serve well.

For example, you might discover a problem you can solve, but when you're devoted to your relationship with God, dependent on the power of God, and determined to make sacrifices for God, it will be the booster rocket that takes your efforts to an entirely different level. Without a *relationship with God*, your vision for solving a problem won't move beyond the temporal (and your motives might be wrong). Without the *power of God*, your service will be limited to your own strengths and wisdom. And if you don't make *sacrifices for God*, your efforts will stop at the edge of Easy Street. The same is true if you want to meet a need, help a person, or create beauty.

Hal Donaldson identified a need he could meet and a problem he could solve when he started Convoy of Hope. But he didn't stop there. He lives each day in the significance sweet spot. He has cultivated a *relationship with God* through faith in Christ. After having dinner with Hal and a small group of pastors, I saw the undeniable sincerity of his faith. He is humble, authentic, and deeply committed to God. His faith in Jesus is the defining relationship of his life, and that relationship is the source of a vision with eternal values, pursued with pure motives.

> *Think of it like the merging of a place and a posture. In other words, the five questions help you determine the place where you can serve. The significance sweet spot helps you develop the posture to serve well.*

Hal also leans on the *power of God*. There were times when he wanted to throw in the towel on Convoy of Hope because of the difficulties and challenges he faced. But time and again God has come through, met their needs, and expanded their impact. When there was simply no human answer, God would show up with a miracle of provision.

Finally, Hal makes meaningful *sacrifices for God*. He left the security of a journalism job, drained his savings account, and took big risks to see Convoy of Hope become what it is today. This organization wasn't founded on Easy Street, nestled in a cul-de-sac of comfort, and hidden under the shade trees of luxury and wealth. It was born out of sacrifice.

Again, your story will look different than Hal's, but God is still intent on using you to advance a mission that He's uniquely gifted you to do. If your life is *outwardly* focused and *upwardly* and *inwardly* aligned, you'll quickly discover where and how you can make your greatest impact. Let me close by reminding you that life is brief. David prayed, "Lord, remind me how brief my time on earth will be. Remind me that my days are numbered—how fleeting my life is" (Psalm 39:4). The number of our days have been counted, and therefore, we must make them count today, and for eternity.

Chapter 13
Focus
Prioritize Your Mission Daily

One of my top five strengths on the CliftonStrengths assessment is *Focus*. "People strong in the Focus theme can take a direction, follow through and make the corrections necessary to stay on track. They prioritize, then act."[84] Even with this strength, I feel the constant tug of distraction. Disruptions and interruptions are everywhere, and it's easy for my *highest priority* to become deluded or sidelined.

In his book *essentialism*, Greg McKeown explains the history of the word "priority." He writes that when "priority" came into the English language in the 1400s, it was singular, not plural. It meant the very first or prior thing, and it stayed singular for 500 years. It wasn't until the 1900s that we pluralized the term and began talking about *priorities*. McKeown observes that we illogically reasoned by changing the word we could bend reality and have multiple "first" things.[85]

We see this principle of staying focused on the first thing (the one thing) throughout Scripture, whether it was Nehemiah building the wall around Jerusalem, or Jesus remaining focused on his mission to preach good news. But one of my favorite examples is Jesus' encounter with two sisters, Mary and Martha. The Gospel of Luke records the encounter: "As they continued their travel, Jesus entered a village. A woman by the name of Martha welcomed him and made him feel quite at home. She had a sister, Mary, who sat before the Master, hanging on every word he said. But Martha was *pulled away* by all she had to do in the kitchen" (Luke 10:38-40a, MSG, emphasis added). Those two words—"pulled away"—so often describe the condition of our lives today.

We're pulled away by projects and people.

We're pulled away by a calendar that is out of control.

We're pulled away by the tyranny of the urgent.

So, how does Martha respond to her state of urgency? She does what many of us do in these high-pressure moments—she complained. "Later, she stepped in, interrupting them. 'Master, don't you care that my sister has abandoned the kitchen to me? Tell her to lend me a hand'" (Luke 10:40, MSG).

Doesn't that sound just like a spoiled niece or nephew, or maybe that bratty kid you used to babysit? If you just switch the names and tweak the situation, you've heard this complaint a hundred times.

Get the picture: Martha storms in, interrupts Jesus' "coaching session" with Mary (and whoever else was in the room) and says, "Jesus, don't you care that I'm stuck in the kitchen. Tell my lazy sister to get in here and help me make some biscuits."

Martha is frustrated, *so frustrated* that I don't think she considered the first four words that came out of her mouth—"Master, don't you care..."

Let's see.

The One who had just fed 5,000 people.

The One who healed the sick, delivered the possessed, and raised a widow's son from the dead.

Jesus obviously doesn't care.

Now, I'm sure Martha didn't mean what she said, but one thing is for sure—Martha's perspective was off, and Jesus pointed it out. "Martha, dear Martha, you're fussing far too much and getting yourself worked up over nothing" (Luke 10:41, MSG). In other words, "Martha, you're busy...so busy that you're missing the point."

> **How often do we forget that being with Jesus is more important than working for Jesus?**

How often do we do the same? How often do we forget that being with Jesus is more important than working for Jesus? How many times do we work *for* a company, work *for* our families, work for our communities (all in the name of Jesus), but we forget to *be with* the One we're working for. That's what Martha was doing. So, Jesus puts it all in perspective with these words: "One thing only is essential, and Mary has chosen it—it's the main course, and won't be taken from her" (Luke 10:42, MSG).

The problem we have in our culture is that we've made everything important, and therefore nothing is important. We've made everything a priority, and therefore nothing is a priority. We have multiple "first" things. We've lost our focus. But "priorit*ies*" is not how Mary approached Jesus. Time with Jesus was Mary's *one* thing. It was her *essential* thing—even though it wasn't the *popular* thing. According to the cultural norms of the day, women were allowed to observe but never participate. They couldn't even be taught the Torah (the first five books of the Old Testament).

> **Sometimes, in the flurry of capturing *the moment*, we actually miss the beauty of the moment.**

But what does Mary do? She trades the norms of culture for the words of Jesus. In fact, on three different occasions Mary sat at Jesus' feet. She learned from Jesus (Luke 10:39), found comfort in Jesus (John 11:31-32), and worshiped Jesus (John 12:2-3). For Mary, sitting at Jesus' feet wasn't just *a* thing; it was the *main* thing. He was the *Main Course*.

What was Jesus saying?

"Martha, the food you're preparing is good, but it's not the main course. I am the Main Course, Martha. Being *with me* is the main course."

When you go to a restaurant and it takes them a long time to bring out the main course, what do you do? You fill up on appetizers. You eat another loaf of bread, or a couple more baskets of chips and salsa. Then, by the time the main course gets to you, you're not even hungry anymore. Martha was doing the same thing. Her preoccupation with the appetizer caused her to miss the main course. She was so busy in the moment that she missed the *moment*.

It's kind of like taking pictures with your cell phone. How many times have you gone to a sporting event, or a concert, or a wedding, and the entire time the crowd has their phones in the air taking pictures? Sometimes, in the flurry of *capturing* the moment, we actually miss the *beauty* of the moment. Each and every day we have an opportunity to enjoy a moment where our souls find rest in the presence of Jesus, but if we're not careful, our busyness will silence the moment.

We'll lose focus.

The temporal will usurp the eternal.

The busyness of life will rob us of the main course.

The Focus Funnel

Like Martha, the apostle Paul surely faced distractions. But like Mary, Paul kept Jesus as the Main Course. He said, "I don't mean to say that I have already achieved these things or that I have already reached perfection. But I *press on* to possess that perfection for which Christ Jesus first possessed me" (Philippians 3:12, emphasis added). How did Paul stay focused on his goal of knowing Christ and making him known? This passage gives us four clues. I like to describe them as a "Focus Funnel."

1. Reality: Recognize Your Present

The focus funnel begins with our present reality. Max DePree once said, "The first responsibility of a leader is to define reality." Whether you're a leader or not, that's good advice, and that's the first step Paul took to stay focused. He acknowledged, "No, dear brothers and sisters, I have not achieved it…" (Philippians 3:13a). Achieved what? His goal of fully knowing Christ.

Why is defining reality so important? Understanding reality helps you identify the gap between where you are, and where you want to be. It shows you how far you've come, and how far you have left to go. If you want to meet a need, solve a problem, help a person, or create beauty in the world, you need to understand your starting point, your current reality.

2. History: Release Your Past

The second layer in Paul's focus funnel was to make sure he wasn't blindsided by his past. He said, "...but I *focus* on this one thing: *Forgetting the past...*" (Philippians 3:13b, emphasis added). What in Paul's past did he need to forget? Two things: his success and his failure.

As I've already mentioned, Paul chose to let go of his success—as defined by his heritage, achievements, and reputation—so that he could pursue his mission of knowing Christ and sharing His message. If I had to guess, Paul's history with other religious leaders probably tried to distract him more than once, but he refused to give in.

Similarly, Paul also had to let go of his history of failures. In his first letter to the Christians in Corinth, Paul said, "For I am the least of all the apostles. In fact, I'm not even worthy to be called an apostle after the way I persecuted God's church" (1 Corinthians 15:9).

Why would Paul say such a thing? Because before he became a follower of Jesus, Paul was persecuting Christians and having them put to death. The weight of that regret

Rather than letting yesterday's distractions become the background noise of your life, choose to release the past so you can focus on what matters today.

must have been unbearable at times, but Paul didn't let it rob his eternal focus. He humbly, yet confidently, declared, "I'm forgetting the past."

You will have to make the same choice.

You can't give the pain of your past authority over today's priority. You can't allow yesterday to have veto power over your mission. Yesterday's success (no matter how glorious it might be), or yesterday's failure (no matter how miserable it might look), should never hold the keys to your daily goal. Rather than letting yesterday's distractions become the background noise of your life, choose to release the past so you can focus on what matters today.

3. Clarity: Restate Your Goal

Once you define reality and release your past, move to the third layer in the focus funnel: restate your goal. Paul said, "I *focus* on this one thing: Forgetting the past and *looking forward to what lies ahead*"

(Philippians 3:13c, emphasis added). Another translation says, "I've got my eye on the goal…" Paul refocused on his eternal mission: knowing Christ and making Him known. He even said that he gave up the "inferior stuff" so he "could know Christ personally" (Philippians 3:8b-11, MSG).

As I've already said, significance starts with an outward focus by determining your need to meet, problem to solve, person to help, or beauty to create. So, why not turn this outward focus into a clear goal: an eternally focused mission that's greater than all the inferior stuff of your past? You'll overcome the inferior parts of your life with a superior goal (one that's motivated by the eternal rather than the temporal). When you put that goal (your mission) in writing, it helps you stay focused.

4. Strategy: Refine Your Plan

Paul said, "I *press on* to reach the end of the race and receive the heavenly prize for which God, through Christ Jesus, is calling us. Let all who are spiritually mature agree on these things. If you disagree on some point, I believe God will make it plain to you. But we must *hold on to the progress* we have already made" (Philippians 3:14-16, emphasis added). What does it look like to "press on," especially when the going gets tough? It requires a strategy so we, like Paul, can make "progress." This is the final part of the focus funnel.

Gail Matthews, a professor at Dominican University of California, provides some helpful insights from her research that show us a strategy to make progress with our goals. She recruited 267 people from a diverse set of professions and nationalities, and then randomly organized them into five different groups. The first group was asked to simply *think* about their goals. They had to determine what they wanted to accomplish over the next four weeks, and they were asked to rate each goal with a variety of metrics. The other four groups wrote their goals down. In addition, the third group identified action commitments, the fourth group also sent their goals to a supportive friend, and the fifth group also provided their supportive friend with weekly progress reports.

What were the results after only four weeks? By only writing goals down, 43% of group one accomplished their goals or were at least halfway there. That's why restating your goal in writing is so important. It clarifies your thinking and turns mental wishes into actionable words. However, 76% of those in the fifth group—that employed action commitments, a supportive friend, and weekly progress reports— accomplished their goals or were at least halfway there.[86]

If you want to remain focused on an eternal mission, it's critical that you refine your strategy to reach your goals. Write your goals down, develop an action plan, and find supportive friends who will walk with you in the journey. This process will help you stay focused.

Easy Street has one focus: comfort. But if you're going to pursue a mission that matters, you have to focus on your goal, even when it feels overwhelming. Let me remind you of Mark Buntain's words to Hal Donaldson in the last chapter. When Hal asked Mark how he and his wife Huldah kept from getting overwhelmed, Mark said, "We stay focused on what we can do—not what we can't."[87] Don't worry about what you *can't* do; instead, focus on the things you *can* do—that matter today and for eternity.

Chapter 14
Mentors
Seek Wisdom for Your Mission

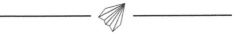

I f you're going to trade the temporal for the eternal, you can start by letting go of any short-sighted definitions of success and choosing your path of significance. Sometimes this means leveraging your current success for a greater purpose, while other times it means completely descending the ladder of success and climbing a new ladder all together. Either way, you'll discover the path to significance when you look outwardly and find a need to meet, a problem to solve, a person to help, or beauty to create. Then, you can align your life upwardly and inwardly by living in the significance sweet spot. This happens by cultivating a relationship with God, leaning on the power of God, and making sacrifices for God that will advance your mission.

This entire process is the route to teach you to step fully outside of Easy Street and live on mission with God. But to make this trade-off, you'll need the help of others. That's where mentors come into the picture. No matter how good you are, mentors will help you get better and go farther.

The word "mentor" comes from ancient Greek literature. "In Homer's epic *The Odyssey*, Odysseus was away from home fighting and journeying for 20 years. During that time, Telemachus, the son he left as a babe in arms, grew up under the supervision of Mentor, an old and trusted friend."[88] That's what mentors are today—trusted advisors who believe in us and invest in us.

Mentors can also serve as coaches. In his book, *Aspire*, Kevin Hall describes the origin of the word "coach." There was a village named "Kocs" in old Hungary that produced horse drawn vehicles to comfortably carry royalty over the bumpy road that connected Budapest and Vienna. These carriages came to be known as "coaches," borrowing their name from the small township where they were designed. Their comfortable design was a superior mode of transportation in fifteenth century Europe, and eventually the term "coach" was applied to the "stagecoach," railway coach, and motor coach. Hall observes, "But however far-reaching and prevalent the word has become since the first coach rolled out of production in Kocs, the meaning has not changed. A 'coach' remains something, or someone, who *carries a valued person from where they are to where they want to be.*"[89]

I have benefited from multiple mentors and coaches as they've helped me move from where I was to where I wanted to be. For example, several years ago, I participated in a coaching cohort in Atlanta, Georgia with several other pastors. Each month I flew to Atlanta for an all-day meeting where we discussed everything from leadership to strategic planning to team development.

To maximize my time in Atlanta, I also I tried to connect with other leaders in the area for short, one-time coaching sessions. I started with Steve Moore, a friend whom I hadn't seen in several years. He's a great leader, and his biblical understanding of leadership is outstanding. In addition to gleaning some fantastic insight, I also asked Steve if he could connect me with a friend of his that was well-known for his leadership expertise. He agreed, and a meeting was scheduled during one of my Atlanta visits. That 90-minute meeting was beyond valuable, but it never would have happened if Steve had not sponsored me into that coaching relationship.

But it didn't stop there.

At the end of my meeting with this individual, I asked him who he knew that I should connect with. He told me about a friend in the area that was starting a coaching organization, and he offered to make an introduction. That introduction led to a nine-month coaching relationship with Shawn Lovejoy. Shawn's insights made an incredible impact on my life and leadership. During this season, I benefited immensely from four different coaching and mentoring relationships, all of which helped me go further in my leadership journey.

Paul the Mentor

The apostle Paul understood the power of mentoring when he said, "Dear brothers and sisters, pattern your lives after mine, and learn from those who follow our example" (Philippians 3:17). Notice the two words Paul used to describe mentorship: "pattern" and "learn." If we're going to benefit from a mentor, we must actively *learn* from the mentor, and we should *pattern* our lives after the mentor's areas of strength. One without the other makes the mentoring process incomplete.

The Message captures Paul's words with fresh perspective, and these words are the foundation for this book. Paul said, "Stick with me, friends. Keep track of those you see running this same course, headed for this same goal" (Philippians 3:17, MSG). Paul displayed a life worth following, and he invites us to stick with him. But then he offers a clear warning of what kind of people to avoid: "There are many out there taking other paths, choosing other goals, and trying to get you to go along with them. I've warned you of them many times; sadly, I'm having to do it again. *All they want is easy street.* They hate Christ's Cross. *But easy street is a dead-end street.* Those who live there make their bellies their gods; belches are their praise; all they can think of is their appetites" (Philippians 3:18-19, MSG, emphasis added).

> *I believe a good mentor offers three gifts:* **pattern, perspective, *and* permission.**

One clear sign of a bad mentor is someone consumed with their own appetites. They choose "other paths" and pursue "other goals" that are actively opposed to the cross of Christ. Paul never wanted followers of Jesus to be mentored in the ways of "easy street," since "easy street is a dead-end street." He hoped that his followers would find mentors to lead them down a path of significance. How do you know if a mentor offers true value? Consider their gifts.

The Gifts of a Mentor

What gifts does a healthy mentor offer to those whom he or she mentors? What gifts do you find in people who will help you resist the lure of easy street and pursue a life of significance? I believe a good mentor offers three gifts: *pattern, perspective,* and *permission.*

First, a healthy mentor models a *pattern* of healthy behavior. Simply put, they model what matters and they practice what they preach. With humility, they can join Paul in saying, "pattern your lives after mine." If you can't trust the character of a mentor, you won't be able to fully trust their coaching.

Second, a good mentor gives you wise *perspective* on the issues you are currently facing. Sometimes the mentor draws that insight out of you by asking good questions. Other times the mentor taps their own well of tested experience and gives you the wisdom you need to free yourself, embrace a better strategy, and navigate your situation. Whatever the approach, a good mentor's perspective is always rooted in wisdom.

Third, a good mentor gives you *permission* to move forward. Shawn Lovejoy helped me understand this gift. It's not that you literally need a mentor's permission before you can act; rather, a good mentor knows how to give you a boost in confidence. They help you believe in yourself and in your mission. They help you silence the voice of self-doubt. They boost your trust in God and refocus your heart on His faithfulness. That confidence boost gives you the courage you need to move forward.

> *Rob Ketterling: "Our relational circle has an effect on the direction and speed of our lives."*

Author and pastor Rob Ketterling wisely observed, "Our relational circle has an effect on the direction and speed of our lives."[90] All friends push you farther, faster. The only question is, which direction are they pushing you. If you want your life to count today—and for eternity—you need to glean the gifts of a wise relational circle. That starts by finding the right mentors who will positively impact the direction and speed of your life.

Six Questions to Help You Find a Mentor

Many people desire to connect with a mentor—they just don't know where to start. Others are able to find a mentor, but they don't know how to maximize the relationship. To find and maximize a mentoring relationship, ask yourself these six questions.

1. What are my growth needs?

Each one of us has unique needs specific to the moment of our life. Those needs are usually connected to a problem, a relationship, a work-related issue, a goal, or some other important area. Similarly, you'll have needs when it comes to pursuing your God-given mission. Before you try to connect with a mentor, identify your greatest growth needs right now. One way to pinpoint your growth needs is to reflect back on the Growth TRAC we discussed in chapter two.

2. Who can help me grow?

Once you understand your growth needs, you'll be better equipped to know what kind of mentor can help you. If you're trying to meet a specific need, solve a problem, help a person, or create beauty in the world, you need mentors that are experienced in those areas. Begin by making a list of everyone in your relational circle, and beside each name jot down the one or two areas where they offer the greatest expertise or experience. Then, pick the mentor (or mentors) you want to pursue who possess wisdom that matches your growth needs.

3. When will I ask?

Once you've identified the mentors you want to pursue, initiate contact with them. What do you say? Let me first tell you what not to say. Don't say, "Hey, I'm looking for someone to mentor me. Would you be willing to help?" That question is too open-ended, and the like-lihood of somebody saying yes is low. Instead, briefly share with the person your desire to grow in a specific area of your life. Then, tell them how much you respect their expertise and experience in that particular area. Finally, ask them if you could buy them a cup of coffee so that you could ask them a few questions in their area of expertise. Promise them you'll keep the meeting to no more than one hour and let them know you'll be glad to email your questions to them in advance. You'd be amazed at how many times the person you ask will say, "Yes! I'd love to help."

Why? Because *your ask shows honor.* It shows honor for their expertise (you're focusing on their strengths), and it shows honor for their time (you're only asking for one 60-minute meeting). Plus, the fact that your desire for growth is driving your request tells the mentor that it will be time well-invested.

4. What will I ask in the meeting?

Being prepared for a mentoring meeting is extremely important.

You're not getting together to "shoot the breeze," you're getting together to grow. That means you need a long list of clear, thought-provoking questions. I say "long list" because if I have 60-minutes, I'd rather run out of time than run out of questions. It's not uncommon for me to have a list of 20-30 questions, knowing that I'll probably only have time to ask five to ten. That's okay. Make your list and then prioritize it. After a brief introduction (if you're new), or a brief time to catch up (if you've known the person for a while), jump into your list of questions.

As you ask questions, be sure to do two things. First, take notes. You won't remember everything they say, and taking notes shows a high level of respect for their wisdom. Second, finish on time. Doing so not only proves that you're a person of your word, but it also increases the potential for a second meeting. If the meeting goes extremely well, and the mentor seems open to continued dialogue, you might say, "As I implement the insights you've shared with me today, would it be okay if I emailed a follow-up question if I hit a sticking point?" They'll most likely say yes, and they might even offer to meet with you again.

5. How will I bless the mentor?

You should always invest back into your mentor. In other words, "How will you bless the person who has just helped you grow?" Simply put, what will you do to say thank you? When I have a one-on-one meeting with a mentor, sometimes I'll give them a small gift such as a book that I've found particularly helpful. Other times I'll ask, "What do I owe you for your time today?" or "What can I do to say thank you for investing in me today?" On one occasion a mentor told me about a mission project he was a part of, and he asked me to consider giving an offering to it. I did.

6. What will I do with what I learned?

The purpose of mentoring is not just to acquire knowledge. Remember, Paul told the believers, "pattern your lives after mine." The ultimate goal is application and transformation. When I'm engaged in longer-term mentoring relationships, I like to start our meeting by telling the mentor what I did with what I had learned from our previous meeting. This lets the mentor know that he's not wasting his time, and that I highly value the relationship. Beyond personal application, one of the greatest things you can do is pass the lessons you've learned on to others. This allows their mentorship to multiply.

Dr. Shirley Peddy observes that, "A mentor's principal purpose is to help another develop the qualities he needs to attain his goals–without a mentor."[91] Mentors don't view themselves as a life-support system for their mentee. Their goal is that the individual can ultimately thrive without them. Their goal is to be one car in the train that successfully transports the person from where they are to where they want to be.

> **Mentors don't view themselves as a life-support system for their mentee. Their goal is that the individual can ultimately thrive without them.**

To trade the temporal for the eternal, you need mentors to help you along the way. Some of these mentors will be intensive, ongoing relationships. This describes my coaching relationship with Shawn Lovejoy (whom I mentioned earlier). Shawn is a professional coach that has helped hundreds of pastors and leaders go to the next level. Other mentors will be occasional or one-time meetings. A couple of the personal examples I shared above fall in this category. Regardless, all good mentoring relationships are valuable.

Finally, if you don't feel like you have a broad enough relational network to get the mentoring you need, start with *distant mentors*. Distant mentoring happens when you allow others to mentor you through their books, resources, and teachings.

Whatever your source of mentoring, make it an ongoing priority. You'll never outgrow your need for a coach or mentor; when you choose to stop chasing easy, you'll always face new challenges. Don't rest on your own pool of wisdom and experience to navigate those challenges. Instead, connect with mentors who will believe in you and help you grow to your full potential. Their investment into your life will equip you to make life count today—and for eternity.

Chapter 15
Heaven
Remember Your Eternal Home

S everal years ago, a heated election was in full swing in our country. The truth is, lately they all seem to be heated. The congregation I pastor has a wide diversity of political persuasions, so I'm always careful to not use the pulpit to promote one party over another. Besides, the Gospel is not under any political party.

During this particular year, I knew, regardless of the election's outcome, that half of our congregation would be celebrating while the other half was fuming. Therefore, I prepared to pastor our congregation through the outcome the Sunday following the election.

After a time of worship that Sunday morning, I stood before our congregation and acknowledged the election. I said, "Some of you today are celebrating the outcome of the election, and others of you are discouraged, depressed, even angry at the outcome." I wanted both sides to know that I acknowledged their feelings. But then I gently reminded everyone (whether they were for, against, or indifferent to the political winner), that our hope is not in a party, platform, or politician. Our hope is in Christ.

I drew the congregation's attention to the apostle Paul's words in Philippians 3:20-21: "But we are citizens of heaven, where the Lord Jesus Christ lives. And we are eagerly waiting for him to return as our Savior. He will take our weak mortal bodies and change them into glorious bodies like his own, using the same power with which he will bring everything under his control."

Following the service, I had people (from both sides of the political aisle) thank me for my comments. Whether you "won" or "lost," you were reminded that your true citizenship is in heaven. Hebrews 13:14 affirms Paul's words: "For this world is not our permanent home; we are looking forward to a home yet to come."

> **When you know heaven is your home, it anchors your identity *and* prioritizes eternity.**

You might be wondering what your citizenship in heaven has to do with your decision to stop chasing easy. Even more, what does it have to do with your mission? When you know heaven is your home, it *anchors your identity* and *prioritizes eternity.*

Identity: Citizens of Heaven Remember Who They Are

When you are reminded of your true citizenship, you are simultaneously reminded of *whose* you are. That's the primary difference between citizenship on earth and citizenship in heaven. Your citizenship on earth is defined by a *place*—your country. Your citizenship in heaven is defined by a *person*—Christ. When you remember your citizenship, you're reminded of the One in whom your identity is firmly established.

Our culture bombards us every day with messages and labels that are in complete opposition to our identity in Christ. Advertisers remind us of what our lives are lacking, and why we will be happier, more important, or more admired if we just purchase the newest gadget or wear the latest fashion. Similarly, culture pressures us to conform to its values, behaviors, and measurements of success.

But again, that's not the basis of our identity.

Christ is.

I have to remind myself of this on a regular basis. That's why I'll often read to myself a "Daily Declaration" that's grounded in the truth of Scripture. It reminds me of my identity as a citizen of heaven. It's a bit long, but trust me, it's a great way to renew your mind. Here's the declaration I read:

> I am a child of God (John 1:12). I am a friend of Jesus (John 15:15). I am justified by faith and I have peace with God through Jesus Christ (Romans 5:1). I have been

bought with a high price (1 Cor. 6:20), and I am a part of Christ's body (1 Cor. 12:27). I am a saint, and I have been adopted by Father God as His son (Eph. 1:1,5). I have access to God through the Holy Spirit (Eph. 2:18). I have been rescued from the kingdom of darkness and brought into the Kingdom of God, because Jesus purchased my freedom and forgave my sins (Col. 1:13-14). I am complete in Christ (Col. 2:10).

I have the mind of Christ (1 Cor 2:16), and I fix my thoughts on what is true, and honorable, and right, and pure, and lovely, and admirable, thinking about things that are excellent and worthy of praise (Phil. 4:8). I overcome the enemy by the blood of the Lamb and the word of my testimony (Revelation 12:11), and no weapon formed against me will succeed (Isaiah 54:17). Greater is He that is in me than he that is in the world (1 John 4:4). The weapons I fight with are not carnal but have divine power to demolish strongholds (2. Or. 10:4-5). I put on the helmet of salvation, breastplate of righteousness, belt of truth, and Gospel of peace, and I take up the shield of faith, the sword of the Spirit, and pray in the Spirit on all occasions (Eph. 6:13-18).

Jesus is the way, the truth, and the life (John 14:6), and the truth sets me free (John 8:31-32), for he who the Son sets free is truly free (John 8:36). I offer and yield myself to God (Romans 6:13), and I offer my body as a living sacrifice. I am dead to sin and alive in Christ (Romans 6:11). I am free from condemnation because I belong to Jesus Christ, and the Holy Spirit has freed me from the power of sin (Romans 12:1-2). I am chosen by God, and I cannot be accused or condemned, for Christ died and rose again and I am in right standing with God (Romans 8:33-34). God works everything for my good (Romans 8:28), and since God is for me, nobody can be against me (Romans 8:31). I am more than a conqueror through Christ who loves me (Romans 8:37), and nothing can separate me from the love of God (Romans 8:38-39). I have been established in Christ and anointed and sealed with the Holy Spirit (2 Cor. 1:21-22). My life is hidden with Christ in God (Col. 3:3).

I am confident that God began, is continuing, and will complete His good work in me (Phil. 1:6). I am a citizen of heaven (Phil. 3:20), and the evil one cannot touch me (1 John 5:18). God has not given me a spirit of fear, but of power, and of love, and of a sound mind (2 Tim. 1:7). I can come boldly and confidently to the throne of God and find his mercy and grace in my time of need (Heb. 4:16, Eph. 3:12).

I am the salt of the earth and the light of the world (Matt. 5:13-14), and I have received power from the Holy Spirit to be His witness (Acts 1:8). I am a branch of the true vine, Jesus, (John 15:5), and I have been chosen and appointed to produce fruit that lasts (John 15:16). I am the temple of God and the Holy Spirit lives in me (1 Cor. 3:16). I am a new creation in Christ; the old life has gone and new life has begun (2 Cor 5:17). I am an ambassador of Christ, and God is making his appeal to others through me as I carry out the ministry of reconciliation (2 Cor. 5:18-21). I am seated with Christ in the heavenly places (Eph 2:4-6). I am God's workmanship, created in Christ Jesus to do good works, which God prepared in advance for me to do (Eph. 2:10). I can do all things through Christ who strengthens me (Phil. 4:13).

It takes me a bit over three minutes to read that declaration, but it's worth every second. It reminds me of who I am in Christ, what Christ has done for me, and what my identity in Him means. It rejects Easy Street and the labels and lies our culture tries to place on us. When we remind ourselves of our identity in Christ, we remember Who we belong to.

Eternity: Citizens of Heaven Remember What Matters

Every citizen has priorities that consume them. As citizens of earth, our priorities tend to revolve around whatever will make our lives easier. Easy Street is the desired destination of earthly citizens, regardless of which country you live in. In fact, every country has its own version of Easy Street. What's easy for one may even be hard for another.

But as citizens of heaven, we have a different priority. Our priority is eternity, and we look for ways to let eternal values shape our daily activities, especially as it relates to our time, talent, and treasure. When you have a *temporal* mindset, you view your resources from an *ownership* mentality. In other words, you believe that *you own* your time, talent, and treasure, and therefore you manage those resources with *your* interests in mind. But when you have an *eternal* mindset, you view your resources with a *stewardship* mentality. Simply put, you

> **When you have an eternal *mindset, you view your resources with a* stewardship *mentality.* Simply put, you view time, talent, and treasure as a gift from God, and therefore you manage those resources with God's interests in mind.**

view time, talent, and treasure as *a gift from God*, and therefore you manage those resources with *God's* interests in mind. Here are a few questions that will help you do just that:

- TIME: Do you regularly allocate time to be with the Lord? Does your schedule reveal a high priority for important relationships? Do you trust God in the area of time, or do you feel a constant drive to work and perform (in case God doesn't show up)?
- TALENT: Have you taken time to identify the gifts and abilities God has entrusted to you? Have you become stagnant in the growth of your gifts, or do you regularly invest in growing to your full capacity? Do you only use your gifts and abilities for your own benefit, or do you willingly invest them in your church and community?
- TREASURE: Do you view your money and income as your own, or do you recognize God as your ultimate source? Do you manage your money wisely, ensuring that you spend, save, and give in proportion to how God has blessed you? Are you financially generous, following the model of Jesus and

the teachings of Scripture, and is your generosity increasing?

Citizens of heaven recognize that these three resources—time, talent, and treasure—come from the Lord. He owns them and we steward them. When we choose to steward them according to the desires of the Owner, we demonstrate a pattern and priority of life that is consistent with our true citizenship.

Pursuing a "Stop Chasing Easy" Mission

Are you ready to make the trade-off? Are you willing to trade the *temporal* for the *eternal* so that you can invest your life in a mission that matters both today and for eternity? It starts by reframing success and focusing on significance. Significance is only found outside the safe borders of Easy Street. That's where God-honoring missions come to life.

Once the mission is born, you'll need mentors to help you pursue your mission, and you'll need to remain grounded in your true citizenship. *Identity* and *eternity* are the marks of your citizenship that remind you *whose you are* and *what matters most*. When heaven is in focus, your allegiance will be to King Jesus, and you'll reinforce that allegiance with your commitment to trade the temporal for the eternal.

To stop chasing easy, you must embrace the right MINDSET, commit to grow your character to MATURITY, and discover the MISSION that will propel you forward. These keys will help you make life count today—and for eternity. But there's one more essential trade-off: MOVEMENT. Movement will help you trade regression for progression.

Part 4: Movement
Trade Regression for Progression

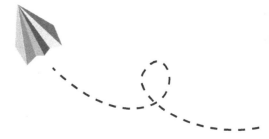

Several years ago, I had a friend who worked in a high-pressure business environment and hated it. Every time I'd see him, I would ask, "How's it going?" And every time he gave me the same one-word answer—"Busy." Eventually he got a better job with a great boss and a great work environment. Each time I saw him, I would ask the same question: "How's it going?" And each time he would give me a one-word answer. But this time the answer wasn't "awesome," or "great," or "amazing." The answer was still the same—"Busy."

"Busy" is the one-word answer lots of us give for our lives. I've been guilty plenty of times. In fact, we wear busyness like a badge of honor. It shows that we can get things done, and it convinces us that we're making progress.

Our "busy" answer begs a better question: are we getting the *right* things done? Are we really making progress, or are we running in circles? John Maxwell, Stephen Graves, and Thomas Addington observed that "Our word *career* comes from two ancient French roots for 'cart' and 'circle.' The word picture is of an individual pushing a cart endlessly in a circle: the treadmill of life."[92] That describes how so many people feel about their lives. They're in a rat race, and each day feels like an endless pursuit of emptiness.

What's the solution? We don't need to stop moving, we just need to adjust our sails and head in a new direction. In other words, we need to align our *movement* with our *mission*.

In the first three parts, we discovered the MINDSET to break out of Easy Street. Then we learned the importance of character, and how MATURITY is essential if we're going to thrive outside of Easy Street. With the right mindset and growing maturity, we then discovered how to trade the temporal for the eternal by adopting a MISSION that truly matters. With that mission in focus, now it's time for MOVEMENT. In other words, we need to trade regression (back to Easy Street), for progression toward the mission God has called us to.

In the next five chapters, I'll share five ways (from Philippians chapter four) to progress toward our eternal mission. It all starts with unity. You can't move forward with a bold, God-inspired mission all alone; you need a unified team to make progress.

Once you achieve unity, you'll have to look fear in the face and courageously say a selfless "Yes" to your mission every single day. Easy Street is cautious, but the adventures outside of its borders are risky. The further you move from Easy Street, the more selfless courage it will take to keep going.

As you pursue your mission, you'll also realize your utter need for God. You'll find yourself staring at larger mountains, facing greater challenges, and fighting bigger spiritual battles. These obstacles often produce anxiety, which is why Paul encouraged us to pray. As we'll discover, prayer not only gives you access to God's help, but it gives you the peace to keep moving forward.

Next, we'll learn the importance of a positive attitude and how to think as we progress toward our mission.

Finally, we'll learn about the uncommon quality of contentment. Contentment seems odd when we're talking about trading regression for progression. In fact, contentment sounds lazy and lifeless, while movement sounds visionary and invigorating. But Paul helps us discover a unique understanding of contentment and how it protects our hearts from unhealthy ambition as we venture into new territory.

We live in a "movement" culture, and yet much of our movement is in the wrong direction. In this final part, we'll learn how to move toward our mission, and how to resist the lure to regress back to Easy Street. Movement is important, but the *way* we progress is even more important.

Chapter 16
Unity
Progress with a United Team

I f you ever went on a long road trip as a kid, there was probably an inevitable conversation that arose. Somewhere in the journey when you were bored out of your mind, you and your brother or sister (or a friend), would draw an imaginary line in the back seat of the car. Neither one of you were allowed to cross *the line*.

It was the boundary.

The territorial dividing point.

The line between *yours* and *mine*.

When I grew up, there were four of us kids, and my parents didn't have a big SUV to cart us around like many families do today. We had one long seat in the back of a green AMC Matador. Imagine going on vacation, driving over 1,100 miles from Texas to Florida, in the back of a Matador. You needed the hope of Disney World—"the happiest place on earth"—just so you wouldn't kill your siblings before you arrived.

Back to "the line."

It always happened.

If your brother wanted to annoy you, he'd slide one finger across the imaginary line. Then you'd mutter, "Stop!"

He'd do it again.

"I said stop!"

He'd wait a minute…maybe two, and then he'd slide his entire hand across the line.

"Dad, Chris won't stay on his side of the line."

A momentary pause, and then it would happen again.

Before you knew it, hands and arms started flailing as the imaginary line completely evaporated.

Suddenly, from the front seat we'd hear, "Do I need to pull this car over?"

That usually put an end to the battle, and the imaginary line was quickly reinstated. By the end of the trip, kids were on the seat, the floorboard, or climbing over the front seat to sit in Mom's lap. Backseat seatbelts weren't a high priority in those days.

Erasing the Lines

Unfortunately, the imaginary lines from our childhood aren't so imaginary anymore. Everywhere you turn, people are fighting, bickering, and posting about anything and everything that divides us. One scroll through your favorite social media channel and you're inundated with finger pointing, unfiltered opinions, and a total loss of civility.

Territorial lines were apparently an issue in Paul's day too. He begins chapter four by unapologetically tackling the issue of disunity. He writes, "Therefore, my dear brothers and sisters, stay true to the Lord. I love you and long to see you, dear friends, for you are my joy and the crown I receive for my work. Now I appeal to Euodia and Syntyche. Please, because you belong to the Lord, settle your disagreement. And I ask you, my true partner, to help these two women, for they worked hard with me in telling others the Good News. They worked along with Clement and the rest of my co-workers, whose names are written in the Book of Life" (Philippians 4:1-3).

Can you imagine what it must have been like when this letter was read to the church in Philippi. I can picture Euodia sitting on one side of the room nodding her head in agreement as the letter was being read. I can picture Syntyche on the other side of the room "amen-ing" Paul's words of instruction. That is, until the person reading the letter got to the part where Paul tells Euodia and Syntyche to "settle their disagreement."

At that moment, one wide-eyed teenager in the room probably started snickering with his friends. And a group of women in the church all looked at each other with whispers, "Thank God! Maybe they'll stop gossiping about each other." Had that happened to us, I'm guessing we wouldn't be sending our pastor any social media love after the service.

Why would Paul address disunity from behind prison bars? Because Paul understood that disunity disrupts our mission and our relationships. In other words, when disunity takes root in our hearts (or our homes, churches, or organizations), the mission gets hijacked and the collateral damage is always relationships.

Think about it in marriage. Winning an argument with your spouse doesn't win you anything. It only disrupts the mission of a healthy marriage and dismantles the relationship. In church, promoting personal agendas usually gets in the way of advancing the Gospel. Personal agendas can even divide the church. In a business, a disunified team will always take the organization off mission, and inevitably relationships and team synergy will be destroyed along the way.

> **Winning an argument with your spouse doesn't win you anything. It only disrupts the mission of a healthy marriage and dismantles the relationship.**

Paul challenged Euodia and Syntyche to protect unity for the sake of the greater mission. He called them to erase the territorial lines and settle their differences. Jesus understood this reality too. In John 17:23, this is how He prayed for his followers before going to the cross: "May they experience such perfect unity that the world will know that you sent me and that you love them as much as you love me." Notice, Jesus connected our unity with His mission. It was the only way forward.

The Multiplying Effect of Unity

Unity has a multiplying effect on mission. When one person pursues a mission, the impact is limited to what that one individual can accomplish. But when an entire team unites around a mission, the impact is multiplied.

The early church understood the multiplying impact of unity on its mission. Acts 4:32 says, "*All* the believers were *united* in heart and mind. And they felt that what they owned was not their own, so they *shared everything* they had" (emphasis added). Notice, unity wasn't limited to a small handful of people. ALL the believers were united. As a result, their unity moved them to serve others in the most extraordinary ways. "There were no needy people among them, because those who owned land or houses would sell them and bring the money to the apostles to give to those in need" (Acts 4:34-35).

This same service-oriented unity marked the Christian church in the third century. In 250 A.D., Christians were feeding more than 1,500 destitute people in Rome every day. And when Emperor Julian—an opponent of Christianity—wanted to revive pagan religion in the mid-300s, he couldn't deny the unified impact these believers were having in Rome. He said that Christianity "has been specially advanced through the loving service rendered to strangers and through their care of the burial of the dead. It is a scandal that there is not a single Jew who is a beggar and that the [Christians] care not only for their own poor but for ours as well; while those who belong to us look in vain for the help we should render them."[93] These early believers made an undeniable impact because they were *united* in serving. Unity multiplied their efforts as they pursued a mission far more important than any one person's ideas or preferences.

> **Wisdom asserts that people are more important than opinions. Wise people understand that doing right is more important than being right.**

Protecting and Progressing in Unity

Our mission and our relationships hang in the balance when unity is compromised. That's why the enemy of your soul will do his best to sow seeds of dissension. In those moments, you must confront dissention and division, (including the conflict caused by your own personal opinions) and unify around the mission. You must leave behind the petty disagreements and forego the temptation to argue about every nuanced difference. *Protect unity.*

Where does it start?

With one word: Humility.

All disunity is the result of pride. Our pride demands that we are right, that our way is best, that our idea, insight, or opinion is the most logical path forward. Perhaps we are correct. Yet wisdom asserts that people are more important than opinions. Wise people understand that doing right is more important than being right. To live this truth requires a posture of humility that puts others before ourselves.

Let me remind you of Paul's words in Philippians 2:2-4: "Then make me truly happy by agreeing wholeheartedly with each other, loving one another, and working together with one mind and purpose. Don't be selfish; don't try to impress others. *Be humble*, thinking of others as better than yourselves. Don't look out only for your own interests, but take an interest in others, too" (emphasis added). Notice, Paul's key for "agreeing wholeheartedly" and "working together" is to "be humble." Humility is the cure for disunity.

Unity helps you focus time, energy, and resources in a single direction. Unity turns the eternal mission God has called you to pursue into a collective, shared effort. It transitions the mission from *me* to *we*, and it accelerates forward moment with an eternal impact.

One final thought: bold missions will always repel a handful of people. They'd rather stand guard over the status quo on Easy Street. You'll likely experience resistance from this group. When you do, listen and learn, make adjustments if necessary, but never go backward. You can't sacrifice the future for the sake of yesterday's traditions. Unify people around the mission, and then move forward with wisdom and humility.

Chapter 17
Selflessness
Progress with a Selfless Yes

D r. George Barna, Director of Research at the Cultural Research Center, has noted that only 6% of Americans today hold a biblical worldview, even though seven out of ten Americans claim to be Christians. A biblical worldview refers to "consistently interpreting and responding to life situations based on biblical principles and teaching."[94] Barna's research shows that commonly held values such as civic duty, hard work, humility, faith, family, moderation and the rule of law have been replaced by acceptance, comfort, control, entertainment, entitlement, experiences, expression, freedom and happiness.[95] Notice, at the core of these new values is a bent toward comfort, ease, and self-centered satisfaction.

A similar self-centered culture existed during the apostle Paul's time, but he didn't support this approach to life. In his letter, Paul said, "Always be full of joy in the Lord; I say it again, rejoice! Let everyone see that you are unselfish and considerate in all you do. Remember that the Lord is coming soon" (Philippians 4:4-5, TLB). I find it amazing that Paul wrote "be full of joy" and "rejoice" while he was in prison. That requires a tremendous amount of perspective. If that were me, "rejoicing" would be at the bottom of my prison to-do-list. Paul doesn't end it there. He implored us to live selflessly.

Some translations use the word "gentleness" instead of "unselfish." However, gentleness is translated from the Greek word *epi-eikes*. One author noted that, "commentators consistently insist that the word contains an element of selflessness. The gentle person does not insist on his rights."[96] Paul calls us to be unselfish and considerate in all we do. In chapter seven, we talked about the importance of humble service, but in this chapter, I want to drill down on selflessness, and how it propels our God-inspired mission. J.W. and Angeline Tucker are a perfect example.

Selflessness in the Congo

In 1939, J. W. (Jay) Tucker and his wife, Angeline, followed the Lord's call to the northern part of the Congo. For years, the Tuckers faithfully served as missionaries to the Congo, and in August 1964, after a short furlough back to the United States, they returned to the Congo, despite unrest in the country.

Less than two weeks after their return, the entire family was captured when a group of rebels known as the "Simbas" took control of Paulis, the town where J. W., Angeline, and their three kids were ministering. Jay, along with other hostages, were taken into custody in a Catholic mission.

When Angeline had not heard from her husband for days, she was finally able to call the Catholic mission to inquire about his welfare. It was the day before Thanksgiving, November 25, 1964. The Mother Superior at the mission hesitated when Angeline asked, "How is my husband?" Then she answered in French: "He is in heaven."[97] J. W. had been killed with sticks, clubs, fists, and broken bottles. Then, the rebels threw his body to the crocodiles in the Bomokande River.[98]

Knowing they were in grave danger, Angeline prayed, asking God for protection. Later that day God answered her prayers as a Belgian and American rescue operation brought Angeline, her three kids, and their coworkers safely to the town of Leopoldville.[99]

One might argue that J.W. Tucker's life was wasted. After 26 years of ministry in the Congo there were no known converts in the Mangbeto tribe.[100] But Jay's martyrdom would prove to be impactful.

The Bomokande River flows through the Mangbeto tribe, and when the king of that tribe was distressed about the violence, he appealed to the central government in Kinshasa. The government sent a police officer known as "the Brigadier." Just two months before J. W. was killed, he had led the Brigadier to the Lord.

The Brigadier tried to witness to the tribe but had little response.

Then, he heard about a Mangbeto tradition that said, "If the blood of any man flows in the Bomokande River, you must listen to his message." So, the Brigadier assembled the king and the elders from the village and said to them, "Some time ago a man was killed, and his body was thrown into your Bomokande River. The crocodiles in this river ate him up. His blood flowed in your river. But before he died, he left me a message." The

> J. W.: "God didn't tell me I had to come out, He only told me that I had to go in."

Brigadier went on to share the Gospel, and as he did, the Holy Spirit descended, and people began to fall on their knees as they cried out to the Lord. Many came to Christ that day.[101]

J. W. Tucker's martyrdom led to a revival in the region. "Thousands decided to follow Christ, and hundreds experienced divine healing. It was even reported some were raised from the dead."[102]

Where did it all start?

It began with a *selfless* "Yes" before the Tuckers returned to the Congo.

Prior to their return, a missionary named Morris Plotts had tried to convince J.W. not to go. The civil unrest in the Congo was becoming increasingly dangerous, and the risk was simply too high. But J. W. said, "God didn't tell me I had to come out, He only told me that I had to go in."[103]

One year after J.W.'s death, the political situation in the Congo had stabilized, and missionaries were allowed to return. Glenn Gohr observed, "One might expect that Angeline, overwhelmed by the loss of her husband, would want nothing to do with Congo. But she worked tirelessly to ensure that her loss would be Congo's gain. She declared, 'If Jesus tarries, there should be a wonderful harvest of souls in all of northeast Congo: for we truly believe that the 'blood of the martyrs is the seed of the Church.'"[104]

J.W.'s selfless "Yes" now counts for eternity.

The Enemy of a Selfless "Yes"

Saying a selfless "Yes" to the Lord, and His eternal mission for our lives, always comes with some form of resistance. The greatest source of resistance is fear. Fear of the unknown. Fear of failure. Fear of rejection, humiliation, or retaliation.

Researchers say we are only born with two innate fears: the fear of falling and the fear of loud noises.[105] Or as one man said, "I'm afraid of making a loud noise when I fall." I came face to face with this fear a few years ago when Karen and I visited the Willis Tower in downtown Chicago. The Willis Tower is a 110-story skyscraper—the 8th tallest building in the world. On the 103rd floor is the Sky Deck, which features the Ledge. The Ledge is a glass box that extends 4.3 feet from the side of the building. When I stepped into this glass box, I looked down, 1,353 feet to the street below. And yes, it was uncomfortable. Okay, maybe I was a tad bit terrified. But it's okay, right? Falling is an innate fear.

Unfortunately, we often turn every other fear into an innate fear too, when in fact, they can be *learned* fears. We impose the glass box of fear onto any situation that makes us feel uncomfortable. In the end, our ultimate response is either *fight* or *flight*. We fight the fear, or we run from it.

Flight will always drive you back to the safety of Easy Street. We love Easy Street because we love control. When we can't control things, fear builds, anxiety has the run of the house, and our lives and futures become very uncertain. Simply put, when fear increases our control decreases, creating a gap filled with chaos. It's in that chaos gap where our trust in God is tested, our peace seems to evaporate, and we're tempted to take flight to Easy Street.

Fight, on the other hand, forces you to face your fears so you can move forward. That's what Franklin Delano Roosevelt did when the United States was devastated by the Great Depression. Unemployment was at 25% and families and farmers were losing everything. That's when the newly elected President delivered a speech and uttered those famous words: "Let me assert my firm belief that the only thing we have to fear is fear itself—nameless, unreasoning, unjustified terror which paralyzes needed efforts to convert retreat into advance."

> **Franklin Delano Roosevelt:** *"Let me assert my firm belief that the only thing we have to fear is fear itself—nameless, unreasoning, unjustified terror which paralyzes needed efforts to convert retreat into advance."*

Why was Roosevelt able to deliver such a passion-filled message to the country? Because he had faced his *own* fears and won. When he was 39 years old, Roosevelt was stricken with polio, which left his hands and legs severely debilitated. During his recovery, he developed a fear of fire, scared that he wouldn't be able to escape a fire because of his disability. But he refused to give fear the final authority over his life. Eventually he regained the use of his hands, and he learned to walk again with the help of braces.[106] With courage infused into his heart, Roosevelt was able to challenge the country to "convert retreat into advance."

How to Progress with a Selfless "Yes"

In chapter thirteen, I talked about maintaining focus on your eternal mission. We discussed the importance of saying "No," to keep yourself from getting distracted from what matters most. But "No" is only half the equation. The other half is a selfless "Yes." To keep advancing forward with your mission, you must continually say "Yes" to the necessary steps and sacrifices. These four steps will help you do just that.

1. Identify Your Next Yes

J. W. and Angeline Tucker said "Yes" when they yielded to God's call to the Congo. But their first yes required many more choices to see their mission advance. The same will be true for you. Your first yes made you leave your caution-filled parking space on Easy Street, but every "first yes" requires a "next yes." In other words, once you say yes to God's mission, you'll have to say yes to every step required for that mission to become a reality.

Your next yes might be to take a risk, work a few extra hours, put your money where your mouth is, or learn a new skill. It might be to cast your vision, create a strategic plan, recruit a team, or have a hard conversation. Whatever your next yes is, I can almost guarantee that it will require a selfless act. Don't worry about the hundreds of yeses to follow; instead, focus on one yes at a time. Always look for the next yes. Which yes will help you live out your mission today?

2. Ditch Your Excuses

When your next yes becomes clear, you may be tempted to craft an excuse as to why you shouldn't do it. Our culture speaks the language of excuses now more than ever. Take, for example, CareerBuilder's list of the most ridiculous excuses that bosses have heard from employees who couldn't come to work. Here are their top ten excuses reported by 2,203 hiring managers and HR professionals[107]:

10. Employee just put a casserole in the oven.
9. Employee's plastic surgery for enhancement purposes needed some "tweaking" to get it just right.
8. Employee was sitting in the bathroom and her feet and legs fell asleep. When she stood up, she fell and broke her ankle.
7. Employee had been at the casino all weekend and still had money left to play with on Monday morning.
6. Employee woke up in a good mood and didn't want to ruin it.
5. Employee had a "lucky night" and didn't know where he was.
4. Employee got stuck in the blood pressure machine at the grocery store and couldn't get out.
3. Employee had a gall stone they wanted to heal holistically.
2. Employee caught their uniform on fire by putting it in the microwave to dry.
1. Employee accidentally got on a plane.

Those excuses certainly sound extreme (even funny or bizarre), but how often do we find ourselves paralyzed by our own excuses. "I'm too young." "I'm too old." "I'm not smart enough, rich enough, or talented enough." "I'm inexperienced, incapable, incompetent, or inadequate." The list could go on and on.

Here's the point: If you want to make your life count today—and for eternity—then quit making excuses. I'd rather fail while doing something that matters than sit safely in my comfortable inaction. Unless you want to wake up at the end of your life with a resume of regrets, choose to step up and step out. Be courageous. God will call you and equip you, but He won't move you. Identify your next yes, and then ditch the excuses that are preventing you from moving forward.

3. Act in Obedience

When J.W. and Angeline Tucker decided to head back to Congo, Morris Plotts tried to convince them to stay home. I'm sure Plotts had perfectly good intentions, but J.W. wasn't deterred. Instead, he bent his ear and his allegiance toward God's call. Every dream chaser has a naysayer, and the bigger the dream, the more naysayers it will attract. Some naysayers are sincere and others are demanding and insulting, but you can't put your vision up for sale to the loudest objector. Instead, say a selfless yes by turning your next step into an act of obedience.

I'd rather fail while doing something that matters than sit safely in my comfortable inaction. Unless you want to wake up at the end of your life with a resume of regrets, choose to step up and step out. Be courageous.

4. Employ Integrity and Skill

Psalm 78:72 says, "And David shepherded them with integrity of heart; with skillful hands he led them" (NIV). To advance in any area of your life, you must employ both skill and integrity. The same is true with your God-inspired mission. Without skill, you won't go far. That's why identifying your gift mix (gifts, abilities, skills, knowledge, influence, and resources) is an important step to pinpointing your mission. When you understand how God equips you, you'll be able to employ those God-given tools and progress toward your mission. In addition to skill, you need integrity. An unwavering commitment to integrity will undergird any progress you make with your skills. This potent combo (skill and integrity) will help you live out a selfless "Yes" to your eternal mission every day.

Experiencing Joy

Look again at Paul's words in Philippians 4:4-5: "Always be full of joy in the Lord; I say it again, rejoice! Let everyone see that you are unselfish and considerate in all you do. Remember that the Lord is coming soon" (TLB). Despite the difficulties of his journey beyond the comfort of Easy Street, Paul placed a double emphasis on joy.

Ironically, rejoicing is a common theme throughout Philippians. Paul rejoiced, even when the Gospel was preached by people who had impure motives (Philippians 1:18). He was determined to rejoice, even if it cost him his life (Philippians 2:17). He told his readers quite plainly, "Yes, you should rejoice, and I will share your joy" (Philippians 2:18). And although the future was unclear, Paul said, "rejoice in the Lord" (Philippians 3:1).

Why was Paul able to rejoice during difficult circumstances? Because his life was invested in the worthiest mission: knowing Christ fully and preaching Christ selflessly. His joy was rooted in the Lord, not his circumstances, and as you pursue your mission, you can experience that same joy. Each step of the way will require a selfless "Yes."

Chapter 18

Courageous Prayers

Progress with God's Help

M ost of our prayers are too safe. Whether we like to admit it or not, our prayers usually revolve around making our lives easier, our bodies healthier, and our wallets fatter. There's nothing wrong with asking for God's blessing. In fact, in the Old Testament, a man named Jabez asked God to bless him, and God granted him his request (1 Chronicles 4:10). But that's only one dimension of prayer. We also need to pray courageously.

Courageous prayers are what bring God-given missions into reach. After all, big missions require great help, and without God's help, we'll never realize the mission. Yet big missions also create a certain amount of worry and anxiety since they compel us to step into unknown territory. These new territories always introduce us to new worries. Here's the good news: Paul gives us the key to deal with our worries, even when we're pursuing a big mission.

> *Courageous prayers are what bring God-given missions into reach. After all, big missions require great help, and without God's help, we'll never realize the mission.*

In Philippians 4:6, Paul writes, "Don't worry about anything; instead, *pray about everything*. Tell God what you need, and thank him for all he has done" (emphasis added). Notice, instead of focusing on worry, Paul encourages us to, "pray about *everything*." This "everything" includes your God-given mission, and in your pursuit of a courageous mission you need to pray courageously. Let me encourage you to start with two courageous prayers.

Courageous Prayer #1: "God, Give Me Boldness..."

In the book of Acts, we find one of the boldest prayers in Scripture, and it's tied directly to the early church's mission. Peter and John are preaching the Gospel when suddenly they're arrested by the captain of the Temple guard and thrown in jail. The next morning, they go before the council of rulers, elders, and teachers of religious law in Jerusalem. Rather than pulling back, Peter and John pressed forward. They boldly proclaimed that salvation was found in Jesus alone. Unsure of what to do, the council members finally ordered Peter and John to stop teaching in the name of Jesus and threatened them before finally letting them go.

How did Peter and John respond?

They prayed.

Not for safety.

Not that God would protect them or stop the persecution.

They prayed for *boldness*.

As soon as they were released, Peter and John returned to the other believers and told them everything that had happened. Then, they lifted their voices to God in prayer and asked for the one thing most of us would ignore: boldness. "And now, O Lord, hear their threats, and give us, your servants, *great boldness in preaching your word*. Stretch out your hand with healing power; may miraculous signs and wonders be done through the name of your holy servant Jesus" (Acts 4:29-30, emphasis added).

Who does that? Who prays for greater boldness after your life has been threatened? Peter and John do. And so should we. That's a courageous prayer. That's a prayer that shoots you like a rocket out of Easy Street and into the work and will of God. That prayer is anything but easy.

What was the outcome? "After this prayer, the meeting place shook, and they were all filled with the Holy Spirit. Then they preached the word of God with boldness" (Acts 4:31). Isn't that why the Holy Spirit was given to us. Jesus said, "But you will receive power when the Holy

Spirit comes upon you. And you will be my witnesses, telling people about me everywhere—in Jerusalem, throughout Judea, in Samaria, and to the ends of the earth" (Acts 1:8). God came through on His promise. He answered their prayers and then they preached boldly—despite the threats, persecution, and suffering that would surely come.

What would happen if you started praying for boldness to fulfill the mission God has entrusted to you? Sometimes God calls people to foreign lands to be missionaries in unsafe places (like J. W. and Angeline Tucker who went to the Congo). Sometimes God leads us down a path that isn't safe, isn't easy, and isn't comfortable. That was the case for John and Nancy.

The church I pastor, 7 City Church, supports a church, academy, and medical clinic located in the Kibera slum in Kenya, Africa. Not only is the poverty, stench, and needs in the slum overwhelming, but it can also be dangerous. When we've conducted medical camps, our host has always insisted we have guards because of the volatility of the situation. And yet, into this dangerous environment, John and Nancy—the pastors of the church we support—*volunteered* to go. Why? Because John grew up in the slum and wanted to return with the hope of the Gospel. It's his eternal mission.

Most people who escape the slum never want to go back. But God birthed a vision in John's heart that he couldn't ignore. Was it comfortable? Absolutely not! Was it a vision that would be easy, glamorous, or earn him a big salary? Anything but. And yet, John and Nancy said a selfless "Yes."

John and Nancy have faced many challenges—and dangers—but they faithfully pray, and God powerfully moves. Every week they minister to more than a hundred people crammed into a small worship space. Many of them are widows left behind after their husbands died of AIDS. Many children are orphans, and yet they receive food and education each weekday in the academy. Why? Because one couple prayed and then boldly obeyed what God called them to do.[108]

Your mission may look different that John and Nancy's, but your prayer needs to be the same: "God, give me boldness." You need God to fill you with His Spirit and empower you with boldness to keep moving forward. Easy Street will call you to return to its comfort and security, but God isn't about Easy Street. He's about empowering you with the boldness to make the greatest difference today—and for eternity.

Courageous Prayer #2: "God, Do the Impossible"

The second courageous prayer is found all throughout the Bible as people cry out to God to do the impossible. Let's focus on one example—Joshua. Let me set the stage.

Five Amorite kings joined forces to attack and destroy the men of Gibeon. So, the men of Gibeon sent messengers to Joshua to plead for help. Joshua and his armies left Gilgal and headed to Gibeon, ready to fight the armies of these five kings. That's when God makes a promise to Joshua: "Do not be afraid of them, for I have given you victory over them. Not a single one of them will be able to stand up to you" (Joshua 10:8).

After travelling all night, Joshua took the Amorite armies by surprise. God gave Joshua a decisive victory, and even sent a deadly hailstorm to help, ultimately killing more of the Amorites than Joshua. But two verses stand out in this story more than any other: "On the day the Lord gave the Israelites victory over the Amorites, Joshua prayed to the Lord in front of all the people of Israel. He said, 'Let the sun stand still over Gibeon, and the moon over the valley of Aijalon.' So the sun stood still and the moon stayed in place until the nation of Israel had defeated its enemies" (Joshua 10:12-13a).

That is an impossible prayer. In fact, it goes on to say, "Is this event not recorded in *The Book of Jashar*? The sun stayed in the middle of the sky, and it did not set as on a normal day" (v. 13b). How crazy is that?

Here's what I love about this prayer. It wasn't normal. It wasn't your everyday, "Bless this food" kind of prayer. And it wasn't just bold and courageous—it was *impossible*. In fact, this prayer was so unique that Joshua 10:14 says, "There has never been a day like this one before or since, when the Lord answered such a prayer. Surely the Lord fought for Israel that day!"

What does it take to pray the kind of prayer to make the history books record such a footnote? I honestly don't know. But I do know this—it has to be a prayer that is impossible to accomplish within your own wisdom, power, and resources. It has to be a prayer so big that when it's answered, God alone receives the glory.

How often do we pray those kinds of prayers—the ones we can't answer, even if we tried? Author Ruth Haley Barton observed, "What is the use of praying if at the very moment of prayer, we have so little confidence in God that we are busy planning our own kind of answer to our prayer."[109] I don't know about you, but I've been guilty of doing just that. There have been times when I've whispered a prayer, said "Amen," and then opened my computer to type out my own plan of action (in case God didn't come through).

I shared with you Pastor John and Nancy's story in the Kibera Slums of Nairobi, but let me offer another example. Pastor Ronald Manyala also ministers in Kenya, Africa. I met him while doing some leadership training for a group of pastors during a visit to Nairobi. When he first met me at the airport, he told me a story that reiterates the impossible nature of God.

Ruth Haley Barton: "What is the use of praying if at the very moment of prayer, we have so little confidence in God that we are busy planning our own kind of answer to our prayer."

At the age of ten, Ronald was, in his words, "a serious drunkard" because his mother was a local beer brewer. As a result, getting his hands on alcohol was fairly easy. He told me, "We lacked food but not beer."

One day Ronald drank some beer that was rejected (unfit for human consumption), and as a result, his intestines were damaged. He was referred to India for an operation, but because of his family's poverty, they couldn't afford it. His father callously said, "Let him die. I will give birth to other children."

Thankfully, Ronald survived, but for the next ten years he endured countless visits to the hospital and came to hate all the hospitals, injections, and drugs designed to help him.

One day, Ronald became seriously ill. His wife attended an overnight meeting hosted on New Year's Eve at a local church. Although resistant at first, Ronald later decided to attend as well. That night, the preacher gave an altar call and said, "Someone has been suffering from severe wounds in the intestines for ten years. You have no peace. Please come forward for your miracle."

Ronald was suspicious, and in his words, "feared fake pastors" who created fake miracles. Ronald hesitated at first, and then decided to step forward. The pastor asked him, "Are you saved?" Ronald said, "No!" The pastor said, "Do you want to be saved?" Ronald said, "No!" Then the pastor asked him a question that changed everything: "Do you want to be healed?" Ronald said, "Yes," and then added, "If I am healed, I will be saved." He admitted, "I was testing God." The pastor looked at Ronald and said, "Lift up your hands." Ronald did as he said, but because of his suspicion, he kept his eyes open.

What happened next shocked Ronald. He said, "I saw one hand passing, and lo, I was down for three hours." When he finally woke up, the church was buzzing with noise. Ronald's cousins had shown up, and they were demanding that if Ronald wasn't healed (and instead died), they would punish the pastor. Some of them even had clubs and swords, ready to fight.

When Ronald woke up, the pastor asked him, "How do you feel?" Ronald said, "I am totally healed." His step-brother immediately said, "It's a lie. Tell him to bend down and touch his toes." Previously, Ronald couldn't touch his toes because of the extreme pain in his intestines, but this day was different. Ronald bent down and touched his toes without an ounce of pain.

Then another person said, "Let him jump five times." Again, previously Ronald couldn't jump because of excruciating pain, but he jumped up and down, all the way from the pulpit to the back of the room. When his cousins saw this, they said, "He is healed." That night, five of Ronald's school mates joined him as they all gave their lives to Christ.

When Ronald told me this story, he concluded by saying, "What the doctor could not do and money could not do, Jesus did it for me. And through all of this affliction, my family, father, mother, and brothers gave their lives to Jesus. I am healthy because of Him. He gave me a ministry to serve His people as a pastor. I thank his name because I believe nothing is impossible to him that believes."[110]

> *Don't let your prayers reside under the tent of safety and security. Pray courageously, believing God to do immeasurably more than you can think, ask, or imagine.*

What "sun stand still" miracle do you need God to do? What miracle would propel your mission forward? Don't let your prayers reside under the tent of safety and security. Pray courageously, believing God to do immeasurably more than you can think, ask, or imagine (Ephesians 3:20). Too much hangs in the balance to play it safe and pray it safe. You need God to do what you can't do. Pray, "God, do the impossible."

Then You Will Experience God's Peace

As I already noted, moving forward with your God-given mission might make you feel worried or anxious. That's normal. But we serve a bold God and a miracle-working God, and He can give both to you. So, as you pray, tell God what you need. Ask for his boldness and invite Him to do miracles. As you do, don't just lean on Philippians 4:6, but also embrace verse 7, which says, "Then you will experience God's peace, which exceeds anything we can understand. His peace will guard your hearts and minds as you live in Christ Jesus."

God makes a promise to guard your heart and mind with peace in the middle of all the uncertainties—a peace that is greater than your own understanding. It starts with prayer. The fact that you're pursuing a mission bigger than you should be a reminder of your need for God's help and God's peace. Let that reality drive you to your knees. Ask God for the boldness to keep progressing, and then ask Him to do the impossible for His glory. That kind of prayer not only makes a difference today, but it changes things for eternity.

Chapter 19
Attitude
Progress with a Positive Attitude

On September 12, 1962, over 35,000 people gathered in the football stadium at Rice University to hear President John F. Kennedy deliver a speech that would mark all of time. He highlighted the innovative spirit of man, celebrating great inventions like the wheel, the printing press, the steam engine, electric lights, the telephone, and automobiles and airplanes. Then Kennedy said, "William Bradford, speaking in 1630 of the founding of the Plymouth Bay Colony, said that all great and honorable actions are accompanied with great difficulties, and both must be enterprised and overcome with answerable courage."[111]

Filled with passion and positivity, Kennedy then launched into a bold vision for a race to space. "We choose to go to the moon," Kennedy said. Then he fastened a timeline to his 240,000-mile bold declaration, refusing to settle for a comfortable pace for this difficult task. "We choose to go to the moon in this decade and do the other things, not because they are easy, but because they are hard, because that goal will serve to organize and measure the best of our energies and skills, because that challenge is one that we are willing to accept, one we are unwilling to postpone, and one which we intend to win, and the others, too."[112]

The moon.

In less than eight years.

Not because it's *easy*, but because it's *hard*.

Kennedy's words were no doubt greeted with a wide range of emotions from avid supporters to skeptical naysayers. But bold visions rarely have unanimous consensus among crowds of people. That's why the person sharing the vision must have an unwavering optimistic attitude. If they're not convinced of their vision and compelled by its possibility, nobody else will believe in their vision. Kennedy was both convinced and compelled.

The United States experienced the fruit of that bold vision on July 20, 1969, with the Apollo 11 mission. Neal Armstrong's infamous words still ring loud: "That's one small step for man, one giant leap for mankind." A small step, but one that started with a contagiously positive attitude.

Fix Your Thoughts

Kennedy's belief and positivity were critical elements to the launch of a mammoth mission. That same positive attitude will be necessary if you're going pursue a life that counts. In the first few chapters, I talked about the importance of adopting the right mindset so you can see beyond the comforts of Easy Street. We explored the mindsets of thankfulness, growth, opportunity, the big picture, and perseverance. These five perspectives dislodge us from the rituals and routines that kept us trapped in a safe life of repetitive mediocrity. But the power of thinking positively doesn't end there. It's an essential companion to create ongoing movement toward the fulfillment of your mission.

> *Attitude isn't a one-time moment of victory. It's a daily pattern of thinking that translates into a daily pattern of living.*

The apostle Paul describes the attitude that creates forward movement with these words in Philippians 4:8-9: "And now, dear brothers and sisters, one final thing. Fix your thoughts on what is true, and honorable, and right, and pure, and lovely, and admirable. Think about things that are excellent and worthy of praise. Keep putting into practice all you learned and received from me—everything you heard from me and saw me doing. Then the God of peace will be with you."

Paul begins with these power-packed words: "Fix your thoughts…" The word "fix" describes mental discipline. In other words, attitude isn't a one-time moment of victory. It's a daily pattern of thinking that translates into a daily pattern of living. The rest of your life starts with the thoughts of your life.[113]

Author Chip Ingram compares our thinking to a train. The engine is our thinking, and it pulls three cars behind it: our emotions, behaviors, and consequences. In other words, thoughts influence our emotions, which in turn influence our behavior, and they ultimately produce consequences. For example, Easy Street thinking creates negative emotions, which produce unwise behavior, resulting in devastating consequences. On the other hand, thought that counts creates positive emotions, which produce wise behavior, resulting in fruitful consequences. Our thoughts have a profound impact on the course of our life.[114] As the old saying goes, "Sow a thought, reap an action. Sow an action, reap a habit. Sow a habit, reap a character. Sow a character, reap a destiny." Proverbs 23:7a says, "For as he thinks in his heart, so *is* he" (NKJV).

This raises an obvious question: On what should we fix our thoughts? That's what Paul spends the remainder of verse eight outlining for us. He says, "Fix your thoughts on what is true, and honorable, and right, and pure, and lovely, and admirable. Think about things that are excellent and worthy of praise." Let's unpack each of these qualities.

True. Truth has the power to set us free and transform our lives. Jesus prayed, "Make them [his disciples] holy by your truth; teach them your word, which is truth" (John 17:17). Jesus knew God's Word was true, and that truth has the power to transform our lives into ones that count for eternity.

Honorable. The word "honorable" refers to reverence and worship. In other words, we should set our minds on what is reverent and worthy of worship, rather than the things of earth.

Right. The word "right" refers to righteousness. When our minds are fixed on righteousness, we choose behaviors that honor God, regardless of what our friends believe to be right, or our culture deems to be wrong.

Pure. When something is pure, it's holy. It is not blemished by sin or immorality. Purity of life begins with purity of thought. Paul instructed Timothy, "Do not share in the sins of others. Keep yourself pure" (1 Timothy 5:22b).

Lovely. Lovely is a reference to something beautiful or attractive.

When you fix your thoughts on what's beautiful to the Lord, your heart is filled with gratitude, joy, and peace. You find yourself filled with an attitude of worshipful thanks.

Admirable. Admirable refers to things that are of good reputation or commendable. Admirable things are worth thinking about and talking about, because they inspire our hearts and minds with a vision of a life fully yielded to Christ.

Paul sums up his "thought list" by saying, "Think about things that are excellent and worthy of praise" (Philippians 4:8b). Whatever you focus on will ultimately expand; thinking about the excellent will build more excellence.

Several years ago, I visited an art museum in San Diego. As I walked through the museum, I encountered stunning works of art, many of which included paintings of Jesus, his disciples, and scenes from the Bible. These paintings were hundreds of years old, and the level of detail in each painting was extraordinary. As I gazed at each painting, I found myself whispering prayers of gratitude to God. Because I was fixing my thoughts on something lovely and admirable, the attention of my heart was attuned to the Lord with words of praise. That's the power of "fixing your thoughts."

How to Progress with a Positive Attitude

I tend to lean in the direction of realism more than optimism. Or as a friend once told me, "Realism is pessimism in denial." But attitudes have a contagious nature to them, and if my attitude is bad, I'll risk infecting everyone around me with it. Attitude is a choice, and I get to choose what kind of attitude I'll have, even when my circumstances are negative. As positivity author and expert Jon Gordon says, "Being positive won't guarantee you'll succeed. But being negative will guarantee you won't."

> *Jon Gordon: "Being positive won't guarantee you'll succeed. But being negative will guarantee you won't."*

The good news is, in his letter to the Romans, the apostle Paul gives us a strategy to change how we think. He said, "Do not conform to the pattern of this world, but be transformed by the *renewing of your mind.* Then you will be able to test and approve what God's will is—his good, pleasing and perfect will" (Romans 12:2, NIV, emphasis added). So, practically speaking, how do we renew our minds?

Start by changing your inputs. What you feed your mind will determine the pattern of your thoughts. You have to sever the negative, toxic, and ungodly inputs that are forming unhealthy paths inside of your brain. These toxic inputs might be the music you listen to, the 24-hour news cycle, the endless scrolling on social media, unhealthy relationships, or gossip and slander. If your intake of negativity and toxicity is outpacing your intake of positivity and purity, you'll never get ahead. Close the negative intake valve, and then open wide the positivity valve by drinking in large doses of God's Word, engaging in heartfelt worship, and spending time in prayer. Add to that a daily request for God to fill you with His Holy Spirit. Paul said, "And do not get drunk with wine, for that is debauchery; but ever be filled *and* stimulated with the [Holy] Spirit" (Ephesians 5:18, AMPC). The phrase "ever be filled" implies an ongoing filling of God's Spirit.

As you open the positivity valve, you'll begin to recognize the subtle lies you've been believing. Some of those lies might be, "I'm worthless," "God doesn't love me," "I'm not gifted or talented," or "I'll never overcome this sin." When these lies and labels come to the surface, choose to actively reorient your life around the truth of God's Word.

One practical way to let God's truth shape you is to use the "Daily Declaration" I shared with you in chapter 15. This declaration is based completely on God's Word, and it's a fantastic tool to reorient your thinking around the truth. As I repeat this declaration day after day, I clear a new path in my mind for healthy thoughts to grow.

Take the lies I noted above for example. Rather than telling myself, "I'm worthless," I declare the truth: "I am a saint, and I have been adopted by Father God as his son" (Ephesians 1:1,5). Rather than buying the lie, "I'm not gifted or talented," I declare, "I am God's workmanship, created in Christ Jesus to do good works, which God prepared in advance for me to do" (Ephesians 2:10). Rather than saying, "I will never overcome this sin," I declare, "I am free from condemnation because I belong to Jesus Christ, and the Holy Spirit has freed me from the power of sin" (Romans 12:1-2). There is a truth to replace *every* lie. Once we discover that truth in God's Word, our job is to declare it and repeat it until it defines us.

It's Worth It

I won't mislead you. Changing how you think is hard work. But if you're going to keep moving forward with your God-given mission, you'll have to keep your thinking in check. You'll have to close the negativity valve that convinces you that a life that counts is too hard and it's time to quit. You'll have to trade the lies for truth, and keep your mind focused on the possibilities of a better tomorrow.

Let me remind you: thoughts lead to emotions, which lead to behaviors, which lead to consequences. Unless you want the rotting fruit of regret-filled consequences to hang from the tree of your life, you'll have to train your thinking onto the path of what is true, honorable, right, pure, lovely, admirable, excellent, and praiseworthy.

Yes, it's hard work.

Yes, the deep-worn path of negativity may be settled in your brain, but you can change. Don't regress to the thinking of Easy Street. Instead, pursue a life that counts today—and for eternity—with the right attitude.

Chapter 20
Contentment
Progress with a Spirit of Enough

L ouis Zamperini is known for his extraordinary survival after his plane crashed in the South Pacific during a rescue mission in World War II. It was May 27, 1943, and only three out of eleven crew members survived when their engine blew 800-miles south of Hawaii. For the next 47 days, they floated 2,000 miles on a life raft toward the Marshall Islands. Francis McNamara (the tail gunner) eventually died, leaving Louis and Russell Phillips (the pilot) to fend for their lives.

During their 47 days at sea, Louis and Phil were shot at by a Japanese fighter plane, drank rain water, and barely survived on "the occasional—raw—albatross that landed on the raft and the few fish that sharks didn't get first."[115] The harsh sun was unrelenting, and when they were finally found by the Japanese, they each only weighed 65 pounds.

For the next two and a half years, Louis was tortured and humiliated at prison camps, "much of it doled out by Sergeant Mutsuhiro Watanabe, a psychopathic and vindictive prison guard nicknamed the Bird."[116] The Bird's goal was to beat Louis until he agreed to make propaganda broadcasts for the Japanese. Louis never did.

When the war ended, Louis and Phil returned home. Eventually Louis married Cynthia Applewhite, and yet, despite being married to the love of his life, Louis struggled to find his place. He dealt with post-traumatic stress disorder, drank too much, constantly got into fights, and had repeated nightmares of trying to kill the Bird. His life spiraled downward until he hit rock bottom.

In 1949, everything changed.

He attended a Billy Graham crusade in Los Angeles where he placed his faith in Christ. He stopped drinking, smoking, and fighting, and he never had a nightmare of the Bird again.[117]

Louis exhibited the most extraordinary tenacity and perseverance imaginable. He endured the harshest conditions at sea, and the most horrific torture in POW camps. But he didn't quit. Why? *Perspective.* In his book, *Don't Give Up, Don't Give In*, we capture a glimpse of Louis's perspective when he writes these words:

> *I'm often asked if, given the chance, I'd live my life the same way again. I have wondered about that as well—for about five seconds. When I think of the juvenile delinquency, injuries, torture, and many near-death experiences, the answer is a definite no. That would be crazy. Of course, enduring and surviving those challenges led to many years of positive influence which helped neutralize the catastrophes and eventually delivered great rewards. I've been honored and blessed with impossible adventures and opportunities, a wonderful family, friends, and fans all over the world. That I'd gladly repeat. It's obvious that one part of the story can't happen without the other. And so I accept it. I am content.*[118]

What an extraordinary perspective. Louis said, "I am content," despite the hardship, the torture, and the pain. In fact, he returned to Japan in 1950 to offer forgiveness to the prison guards who had tortured him.

Being content isn't easy. The truth is, contentment feels like a moving target in a culture that constantly tells us, "You don't have enough." Our culture will tell you that you won't be happy until you buy this, own that, or drive one of these. You won't be successful until you graduate from *here* or work over *there*. You won't be fulfilled until you're married, or until you're divorced, or until you upgrade to the newest version. Simply put, supposedly the reason you're not happy, successful, and fulfilled is because you don't have *enough*.

Social media certainly doesn't help the situation. It exaggerates the "not enough" syndrome as you scroll through your feed to discover the party you didn't get invited to, your co-worker (who you don't even like) enjoying a beach vacation, or your friend taking a selfie with your ex-boyfriend. Interestingly, this lack of contentment exists everywhere you go. On Easy Street, lack of contentment shows up quickly because no matter how comfortable you are, it's never enough. Thoughts of more, bigger, and better leave you constantly wanting.

However, lack of contentment is not restricted to Easy Street. It also shows up in our pursuit of a life that counts. How? After we accomplish something great, we find ourselves in a rat race for something greater. Not only do we want more impact, bigger results, and better outcomes, but we want it *now*.

> **Contentment helps us live in the tension between satisfied *and* significant.**

Although yesterday's courage can quickly become today's Easy Street, it's also true that our lack of contentment can make us idolize the pursuit of significance. Contentment helps us live in the tension between *satisfied* and *significant*. Healthy contentment protects our hearts from unhealthy ambition while still preventing us from settling in a new comfort zone. With all of the significance experienced by the apostle Paul, he still learned how to be content. Paul said:

How I praise the Lord that you are concerned about me again. I know you have always been concerned for me, but you didn't have the chance to help me. Not that I was ever in need, for I have learned how to be content with whatever I have. I know how to live on almost nothing or with everything. I have learned the secret of living in every situation, whether it is with a full stomach or empty, with plenty or little. For I can do everything through Christ, who gives me strength. Even so, you have done well to share with me in my present difficulty. As you know, you Philippians were the only ones who gave me financial help when I first brought you the Good News and then traveled on from Macedonia. No other church did this. Even when I was in Thessalonica you sent help more than once. I don't say this because I want a gift from you. Rather, I want you to receive a reward for your kindness. At the moment I have all I need—and more! I am generously supplied with the gifts you sent me with Epaphroditus. They are a sweet-smelling sacrifice that is acceptable and pleasing to God. And this same God who takes care of me will supply all your needs from his glorious riches, which have been given to us in Christ Jesus. *Now all glory to God our Father forever and ever! Amen. (Philippians 4:10-20, emphasis added)*

How did Paul learn to be content? He learned contentment when he realized that *Christ is enough* and *His enough is endless.*

Christ is Enough

When Paul said, "Not that I was ever in need, for I have learned how to be content with whatever I have," the word "content" suggests "self-sufficiency." Why would he choose that word? Because in Paul's day, a group of Greek philosophers known as the Stoics believed that a person's peace and happiness could be found within themselves. In other words, they believed that everything you need to be truly happy—regardless of your circumstances—is found in you. You were "self-sufficient."[119]

When Paul used this word, it would be easy to think he was saying, "I'm content because I'm self-sufficient. *I'm enough.* I've got everything I need within myself. I don't need help from anyone else." But that's not what Paul was saying at all, because in verse 13 he writes, "For I can do everything through Christ, who gives me strength." In other words, "I can do everything, not through *myself* who gives me strength, but through *Christ* who gives me strength." His sufficiency was found in Christ. He learned to be content because Christ is enough.

The Amplified version of Philippians 4:11 captures this well: "Not that I speak from [any personal] need, for I have learned to be content [and self-sufficient through Christ, satisfied to the point where I am not disturbed or uneasy] regardless of my circumstances." Paul was not disturbed or uneasy because true contentment allows you to experience peace in the midst of your problems.

A few years ago, my sister-in-law, Ruth, was diagnosed with cancer and had to have a double mastectomy, but something always struck me about Ruth's experience. She told me that a couple of weeks after she was first diagnosed, she was driving to a women's Bible study when suddenly an overwhelming sense of peace came over her. She said, "I felt like I was behind four-foot thick concrete walls, like a fortress, and fear could *not* get in." This wasn't like her, because Ruth admitted she could go to a place of fear pretty quickly in her life. But for the *first* time, Ruth found herself saying, "Whatever you want to do here, God, I'm good with it…heal me or don't. I want what you want." God did restore Ruth's health, and through her entire ordeal, His peace stayed with her.[120]

Was the cancer disturbing? Sure.

Was the cancer difficult and uneasy? Absolutely.

And yet, like Paul, Ruth found a comforting contentment in the midst of her situation.

Paul's contentment was present in the good times and in the bad times. He said, "I know how to live on almost nothing or with everything. I have learned the secret of living in every situation, whether it is with a full stomach or empty, with plenty or little" (Philippians 4:12). How is that possible? It's possible because Paul came to recognize, "I need God, *period.*" In

> **If I don't need God when times are good, then I've turned my good into a god.**

other words, when times are bad, I need God. But I need God *just as much* when times are good. If I don't need God in the good times, I've become sufficient in myself. Said another way, if I don't need God when times are good, then I've turned my good into a god.

God doesn't play that game.

God doesn't compete.

You have to answer the question, "Is Christ enough for me?" or do I need "Christ *plus.*"

Christ *plus* that new job.

Christ *plus* my good-looking girlfriend.

Christ *plus* a better car.

Christ *plus* the college scholarship.

You will find the strength to live contently in the midst of uncertainty when you resolve that Christ, and Christ alone, is enough. How is that possible? Because Christ's enough is *endless.*

His Enough is Endless

When you hear that "Christ is enough," it's easy to interpret "enough" as "just enough" or "just barely enough." You get the picture of your car rolling into a gas station on fumes. You had *just enough* gas to make it to the station before you were stranded on the side of the road.

That's not the picture Paul paints of Christ. In fact, he almost describes a paradoxical picture of contentment: "And this same God who takes care of me will supply all your needs from his glorious riches, which have been given to us in Christ Jesus" (Philippians 4:19). That word "supply" means to "make full." It's the removal of any deficiency. It's the idea of filling something so completely that there is no room for anymore. Paul was saying, God will supply all of your needs to the point that you can't contain any more.

When you're in a moment of uncertainty, you usually feel deficient or lacking. In other words, you feel like you have just barely enough to make it. But God is full of glorious riches, and out of those glorious riches He is not only able, but willing, to fill you. He leaves no deficiency. He fills you to overflowing. He causes your soul to overflow with His rich and glorious supply. When Paul writes these words, he's reminding us of a promise we have in Christ. He uses three words in verse 19 to describe the completeness of God's supply: "will," "all," and "glorious riches."

First, Paul didn't say that God *might* supply your needs, *should* supply your needs, or *could* supply your needs. He said *God will*. God is faithful to take care of His people. Second, Paul doesn't say God will supply *some* of your needs. Again, God makes full and leaves no deficiency. He supplies *all* of your needs. Third—and this is my favorite part—God is able to supply all of your needs because His supply is not tied to us, but to Him. He's not drawing the supply for our needs from the economy, or the wisdom of people, or from a reservoir that's in danger of drying up. God's *glorious riches* are infinite because God is infinite, and our needs are no match for His ability to supply. You can be content, because *Christ is enough*, and *His enough is endless*. That doesn't mean God will give you every wish and every want. But it does mean He'll meet your needs and provide you with the resources to advance forward in His mission for your life.

Progressing with Enough

Contentment doesn't seem relevant when it comes to pursuing a life that counts both today and for eternity. After all, in our modern-day culture, contentment feels like laziness. It sounds like we're coasting, and that we've lost our passion. In fact, to admit that we're content almost sounds like defeat. But when you understand that *Christ is enough* and *His enough is endless*, you discover the extraordinary relevance contentment has to how you move forward with your mission.

First, your mission will continually expand with greater possibilities the further you get from Easy Street. You'll have new ideas, and fresh visions will enter your mind. You'll begin to see a bigger mission and an opportunity to have greater impact. As you do, you'll be reminded of your lack. You'll be reminded that these new dreams come with real price tags. In those

> *No matter how big and audacious your mission might be, contentment keeps you grounded in the fact that* **Christ is enough.**

moments, remember that there is no shortage in God's infinite supply. Again, *His enough is endless.* If God is birthing new dreams in your Spirit, He is quite capable of meeting your needs so that His dreams for you can become reality.

Second, no matter how big and audacious your mission might be, contentment keeps you grounded in the fact that *Christ is enough.* He alone satisfies. Yes, He will give you fresh vision. And yes, He will lead you into uncharted territory. But a vision of a greater tomorrow can never replace your vision of Christ. At the end of the day, *Christ is enough*, even if all your dreams disappear. You can be content in Him.

The Reward

A common theme in Paul's writings is that of running a race. In Philippians 3:14, Paul described a "heavenly prize" that awaits those who finish the race. Abandoning Easy Street to make your life count for something bigger will not go unnoticed. God rewards the faithful. God rewards the diligent. God rewards obedience.

As the apostle Paul wraps up his letter, he concludes with these words: "Give my greetings to each of God's holy people—all who belong to Christ Jesus. The brothers who are with me send you their greetings. And all the rest of God's people send you greetings, too, especially those in Caesar's household. May the grace of the Lord Jesus Christ be with your spirit" (Philippians 4:21-23).

As you run your race outside the confines of Easy Street, may the grace of the Lord Jesus Christ be with your spirit. My you not run the race in your own strength, power, and wisdom, but in the grace God freely gives. The word "grace" means favor. It's the unmerited favor of God that cannot be earned. His grace saves us and sustains us, and God is faithful to extend His sustaining grace to those who run the race He's called them to pursue.

Stop chasing easy!

Abandon the dead-end street known as "Easy Street."

Trade empty pursuits for a life that counts today—and for eternity.

That trade-off will require the right mindset, maturity, mission, and movement. You'll need to trade pessimism for perspective, comfort for character, the temporal for the eternal, and regression for progression. But when you do, God will go before you, walk beside you, and make a way where there seems to be no way. The reward of Easy Street is fleeting, but the reward for a life in pursuit of God and His will cannot be matched. He is good, and His faithfulness awaits you outside of Easy Street.

Acknowledgments

Thank you Karen for your unwavering love and support throughout this project. This book has been in the works for a long time, and you patiently supported me through each phase of the journey. I love you forever, and I'm so thankful we can make life count together.

Thank you Ashley and Dylan for your words of encouragement. My prayer is that this book inspires you to pursue all God has for you, and that you'll never stop dreaming of the difference you can make in the world. And to Elijah and Wyatt, may you grow up to make each day count for eternity. I love you.

Thank you Mom and Dad for your faithful support through your prayers and words of encouragement. Your faith in God is a testimony to so many, and you inspire others to pursue a vibrant relationship with Jesus.

Thank you to my literary agent, Greg Johnson. You believed in me, and you found a home for *Stop Chasing Easy*. Your wisdom and insight along the journey have meant so much.

Thank you Robert Walker, and the team at The Core Media Group, for publishing *Stop Chasing Easy*. Your gracious support and guidance through the publishing process is deeply appreciated, and your encouragement has made it a joy to work alongside of you on this project.

Thank you 7 City Church for the privilege to serve you as your pastor. May the message of this book inspire you to dream big and pursue Jesus beyond the edges of safety and comfort.

Above all, thank you Jesus for the way you lead us beyond Easy Street into a life of impact. When you call us to trust you, you always prove faithful. The idea for this book was inspired by your Word, and I'm so grateful you continually draw us beyond the walls of ease to pursue a life that counts for eternity.

Notes

Introduction

1. "What Were Roman Prisons Like in Paul's Time," Olive Tree Blog, retrieved July 13, 2021, https://www.olivetree.com/blog/imprisonment-in-the-roman-world/.
2. Louie Giglio, *Goliath Must Fall Video Study: Winning the Battle Against Your Giants,* Session 4. Nashville, TN: Thomas Nelson Inc., 2017. DVD.
3. William Barclay, *The Gospel of Matthew: Volume 2, The Daily Bible Study Series* (Philadelphia, PA: Westminster John Knox Press, 1975), 18.

Chapter 1

4. "Giving Thanks Can Make You Happier," Harvard Health Publishing, retrieved August 14, 2021, https://www.health.harvard.edu/healthbeat/giving-thanks-can-make-you-happier.
5. Joshua Brown & Joel Wong, "How Gratitude Changes You and Your Brain," June 6, 2017, https://greatergood.berkeley.edu/article/item/how_gratitude_changes_you_and_your_brain.
6. Colossians 1:24, NLT.
7. I originally introduced the idea of END Thanks, IN Thanks, and FOR Thanks, and its application to my heart failure, in my mini ebook, *4 Keys to Conquer Anxiety,* 2020, 17-19.

8. I chronicle the journey of my heart failure in a book I co-authored with my wife Karen Blandino, *Unexpected: What to Do When Life Disrupts Your Plans*, 2014.

Chapter 2

9. "Eric Hoffer Quotes," BrainyQuote, https://www.brainyquote.com/quotes/eric_hoffer_109153.
10. I chronicle my journey of reading and personal growth in my book, *GO! Starting a Personal Growth Revolution*, 2012.
11. C.S. Lewis quote, The Pastor's Workshop, retrieved August 18, 2021, https://thepastorsworkshop.com/sermon-quotes-on-learning/
12. Sam Chand, *Leadership Pain: The Classroom for Growth* (Nashville: Thomas Nelson, 2015), 15.
13. I unpack the Growth TRAC model in detail in my book, *GO! Starting a Personal Growth Revolution*, 2012.

Chapter 3

14. Matthew McCreary, "ChIck-fil-A Makes More Per Restaurant Than McDonald's, Starbucks and Subway Combined... and It's Closed on Sundays," Entrepreneur, retrieved July 19, 2021, https://www.entrepreneur.com/article/320615.
15. Abby Ohlheiser, "The World According to Chick-fil-A Founder Truett Cathy," The Washington Post, September 8, 2014, https://www.washingtonpost.com/news/morning-mix/wp/2014/09/08/the-world-according-to-chick-fil-a-founder-truett-cathy/?noredirect=on&utm_term=.f5acc3e3eb97.
16. Dick Parker, "Humble Beginnings," November 11, 2016, https://www.chick-fil-a.com/inside-chick-fil-a/humble-beginnings-how-truett-cathys-love-for-customers-grew-from-a-coke-and-smile.
17. Ibid.
18. "About Chick-fil-A Inc.," retrieved July 19, 2021, https://thechickenwire.chick-fil-a.com/Press-Room.
19. S. Truett Cathy, *Eat Mor Chikin: Inspire More People: Doing Business the Chick-fil-A Way* (Chicago: Looking Glass Books, Inc, 2002), 19-20.

20. Dick Parker, "A Life Centered on Family," August 11, 2016, https://thechickenwire.chick-fil-a.com/Inside-Chick-fil-A/A-Life-Centered-on-Family.

21. S. Truett Cathy, *It's Easier to Succeed Than to Fail* (Nashville: Thomas Nelson, 1989), 58, 60, 61.

22. Cathy, It's Easier to Succeed Than to Fail, 61-65.

23. Cathy, *Eat Mor Chikin*, 4.

24. Ibid, 4.

25. Hal Urban, *Life's Greatest Lessons: 20 Things That Matter* (New York: Fireside, 2003), 12.

26. "5 Whys: The Ultimate Root Cause Analysis Tool," Kanbanize, retrieved July 19, 2021, https://kanbanize.com/lean-management/improvement/5-whys-analysis-tool.

Chapter 4

27. "Eugene Delacroix and His Paintings," Eugene Delacroix: Famous Paintings and Biography, retrieved December 30, 2018, http://www.eugene-delacroix.com.

Chapter 5

28. Brian Tracey, "How To Be Indispensable At Work," Brian Tracey International, retrieved December 31, 2018, https://www.briantracy.com/blog/leadership-success/the-key-to-long-term-success/.

29. Wilbert R. Shenk, "Morrison, Robert," in *Biographical Dictionary of Christian Missions*, ed. Gerald H. Anderson (New York: Macmillan Reference USA, 1998), 473-74.

30. Martha Stockment, "Robert Morrison: Pioneer Protestant Missionary to China," Biographical Dictionary of Chinese Christianity, retrieved December 31, 2018, http://bdcconline.net/en/stories/morrison-robert.

31. Craig Groeschel, The Global Leadership Summit, retrieved August 5, 2021.

32. Shola Richards, The Global Leadership Summit, retrieved August 5, 2021.

33. Angela Lee Duckworth, "Grit: The Power of Passion and Perseverance," TED Talks Education, retrieved December 31,

2018, https://www.ted.com/talks/angela_lee_duckworth_grit_the_power_of_passion_and_perseverance/transcript?language=en.

34. Duncan Larkin, "Conquer the Final Miles of Your Marathon," Motivrunning, October 4, 2017, https://www.motivrunning.com/runner-training/conquer-final-miles-marathon/

35. Patrick McCrann, "How to Beat the Wall During Your Marathon," Active, retrieved January 1, 2019, https://www.active.com/running/articles/how-to-beat-the-wall-during-your-marathon

Part 2

36. Andy Stanley, *Louder Than Words: The Power of Uncompromised Living* (Colorado Springs: Multnomah, 2004), 31.

Chapter 6

37. William Raspberry, quoted by John Maxwell, "Responsibility: The First Step in Learning," John Maxwell, September 20, 2013, https://www.johnmaxwell.com/blog/responsibility-the-first-step-in-learning/.

38. Ruth Haley Barton, quoted by John Maxwell, *Developing the Leader Within You 2.0 Workbook* (Nashville: Thomas Nelson, 2018), 70.

39. Interview with Bob Goff, "Praise," TBN, December 7, 2018.

40. 1 Corinthians 13:4-7, NLT.

41. Romans 12:21, NLT.

42. "Eric Hoffer Quotes," BrainyQuote, https://www.brainyquote.com/quotes/eric_hoffer_152434.

Chapter 7

43. Scott Harrison, "The Charity Water Story," North Point Community Church, July 26, 2017, YouTube, https://www.youtube.com/watch?v=w8QdFdtsmbs.

44. Scott Harrison, *Thirst* (New York: Currency, 2018), 47.

45. Scott Harrison, 52.

46. Ibid, "The Charity Water Story."

47. Scott Harrison, 65.

48. Mercy Ships, retrieved February 2, 2019, https://www.mercyships.org/?_ga=2.13354999.1385574795.1549130521-668792407.1489186319&_gac=1.6382470.1549130521.EAIaIQobChMIwKn68NCd4AIV1f_jBx2kegitEAAYASAAE-gLB3fD_BwE.
49. Scott Harrison, 82.
50. Scott Harrison, 141.
51. Retrieved August 18, 2021, https://www.charitywater.org.
52. Harrison, YouTube.
53. Retrieved August 18, 2021, https://www.charitywater.org/our-work#.
54. John Dickson, *Humilitas* (Grand Rapids: Zondervan, 2011), 24.
55. R.C. Sproul, *Enjoying God: Finding Hope in the Attributes of God* (Grand Rapids: Zondervan, 2017), 30.
56. James 4:6

Chapter 8

57. The story of Stephen and Priscilla Perumalla is used by permission and is adapted from an email sent to the author on March 18, 2019.
58. Judith Viorst, *Alexander and the Terrible, Horrible, No Good, Very Bad Day* (New York: Antheneum Books, 1987).
59. John Maxwell, *The Winning Attitude: Your Key to Personal Success* (Nashville: Thomas Nelson, 1993), 24.
60. For more on God's power to live a life of obedience, see 2 Timothy 1:7, Ephesians 3:20, Philippians 4:13.
61. "Research," Back to the Bible, retrieved February 16, 2019, https://www.backtothebible.org/research.
62. Arnold Cole and Pamela Caudill Ovwigho, "Understanding the Bible Engagement Challenge: Scientific Evidence for the Power of 4," Center for Bible Engagement, December 2009, https://bttbfiles.com/web/docs/cbe/Scientific_Evidence_for_the_Power_of_4.pdf.

Chapter 9

63. Permission granted by Derek Moffatt to share this story on September 1, 2021.

Chapter 10

64. Permission granted by Darius Johnston to share this story on September 7, 2021.

65. For more details on this concept, see the article on my blog at http://stephenblandino.com/2019/09/three-ways-to-lead-faithful-team-members.html.

Chapter 11

66. "Stephen R. Covey Quotes," retrieved August 5, 2021, https://www.goodreads.com/quotes/194341-if-the-ladder-is-not-leaning-against-the-right-wall.

67. "Lewis Carroll Quotes," retrieved August 5, 2020, https://www.goodreads.com/quotes/642816-if-you-don-t-know-where-you-are-going-any-road.

68. John MacArthur, *The MacArthur New Testament Commentary, Philippians* (Chicago: Moody Publishers, 2001), 228-230.

69. Larry Osborne, *Accidental Pharisees: Avoiding Pride, Exclusivity, and the Other Dangers of Overzealous Faith* (Grand Rapids: Zondervan, 2012), 24.

70. John MacArthur, p. 231.

71. "About," retrieved July 12, 2019, https://philvischer.com/about/.

72. "Me, Myself, & Bob Quotes," Goodreads, retrieved August 19, 2021, https://www.goodreads.com/work/quotes/105538-me-myself-and-bob-a-true-story-about-god-dreams-and-talking-vegetab.

73. "Phil Vischer Quotes," Goodreads, retrieved August 19, 2021, https://www.goodreads.com/quotes/8970665-if-god-gives-you-a-dream-and-the-dream-comes.

Chapter 12

74. Hal Donaldson with Kirk Noonan, *Your Next 24 Hours: One Day of Kindness Can Change Everything* (Grand Rapids: Baker Books, 2017), 13.

75. Ibid, 14.

76. Ibid, 14.

77. Ibid, 15.

78. Hal Donaldson, *Disruptive Compassion: Becoming the Revolutionary You Were Born to Be* (Grand Rapids: Zondervan, 2019), 46.
79. Hal Donaldson, *Disruptive Compassion*, 49.
80. Ibid, 16.
81. "About," retrieved August 13, 2021, https://convoyofhope.org/about/.
82. Andy Stanley, *Taking Care of Business Study Guide: Finding God at Work* (Colorado Springs: Multnomah, 2010), 15.
83. Galatians 5:24.

Chapter 13

84. "An Introduction to the Focus CliftonStrengths Theme," retrieved November 1, 2019, https://www.gallup.com/cliftonstrengths/en/252239/focus-theme.aspx.
85. Greg McKeown, *essentialism: The Disciplined Pursuit of Less* (New York: Crown Business, 2014), 16.
86. "Dominican Scholar, Press Releases, Communications and Media Relations," Dominican University of California, February 1, 2015, https://www.dominican.edu/sites/default/files/2020-02/gailmatthews-harvard-goals-researchsummary.pdf.
87. Hal Donaldson, *Disruptive Compassion*, 49.

Chapter 14

88. "Mentor," retrieved November 27, 2019, https://www.merriam-webster.com/dictionary/mentor#note-1.
89. Kevin Hall, *Aspire: Discovering Your Purpose Through the Power of Words* (New York: William Morrow, 2009), 165-166.
90. Rob Ketterling, *Change Before You Have To* (Springfield, MO: Influence Resources, 2012), 92.
91. Dr. Shirley Peddy, *The Art of Mentoring: Lead, Follow and Get Out of the Way* (Houston, TX: Bullion Books, 2001), 24-25.

Part 4

92. John Maxwell, Stephen Graves, and Thomas Addington, *Life@Work: Marketplace Success for People of Faith* (Nashville: Thomas Nelson, 2005), 79.

Chapter 16

93. Ken Curtis, PHD, "The Spread of the Early Church," Christianity.com, May 3, 2010, https://www.christianity.com/church/church-history/timeline/1-300/the-spread-of-the-early-church-11629561.html.

Chapter 17

94. "American Worldview Inventory 2020 – At A Glance," Cultural Research Center, March 24, 2020, https://www.arizonachristian.edu/wp-content/uploads/2020/03/CRC_AWVI2020_Report.pdf.

95. Ibid.

96. R.R. Melick, Philippians, Colossians, Philemon (Vol. 32), (Nashville: Broadman & Holman Publishers, 1991), 149.

97. Glenn W. Gohr, "This Week in AG History – November 21, 1965," November 19, 2015, https://news.ag.org/en/Features/This-Week-in-AG-History--November-21-1965.

98. "A Missionary's Sacrifice Was Worth the Cost," Sermon Illustration, retrieved January 10, 2020, https://www.preaching-today.com/illustrations/2008/august/7032706.html.

99. Ibid. Glenn W. Gohr.

100. Assemblies of God Heritage, Vol. 8, No. 4, Winter 1988-89, 2.

101. Ibid. Preaching Today.

102. Ibid. Glenn W. Gohr.

103. Mark Batterson, Chase The Lion, (Colorado Springs: Multnomah, 2016), 100.

104. Ibid. Glenn W. Gohr.

105. Nadia Kounang, "What is the Science Behind Fear," CNN, October 29, 2015, http://www.cnn.com/2015/10/29/health/science-of-fear/.

106. John Maxwell, The Difference Maker: Making Your Attitude Your Greatest Asset (Nashville: Thomas Nelson, 2006), 121-122.

107. Ben Popken, "Top 10 Most Unbelievable Excuses for Calling in Sick," Today, October 23, 2014, https://www.today.com/money/top-10-most-unbelievable-excuses-calling-sick-1D80234728.

Chapter 18

108. I met John and Nancy during my trips to Kenya in 2018 and 2019.

109. Ruth Haley Barton, *Strengthening the Soul of Your Leadership: Seeking God in the Crucible of Ministry* (Downers Grove, IL: InterVarsity Press, 2018), 145.

110. Ronald Manyala personally shared his story with me during a visit to Kenya, Africa in June 2019.

Chapter 19

111. "John F. Kennedy Moon Speech – Rice Stadium," September 12, 1962, retrieved July 13, 2019, https://er.jsc.nasa.gov/seh/ricetalk.htm.

112. Ibid, John F. Kennedy Moon Speech.

113. I originally introduced the description of "fix" from Philippians 4:8-9 in my mini ebook, *4 Keys to Conquer Anxiety*, 2020, 21.

114. Chip Ingram, *Good to Great in God's Eyes: 10 Practices Great Christians Have in Common* (Grand Rapids: Baker Books, 2007), 15.

Chapter 20

115. Louis Zamperini and David Rensin, *Don't Give Up, Don't Give In: Lessons from an Extraordinary Life* (New York: Dey Street Books, 2014), XXII.

116. Ibid, XXIII.

117. Ibid, XXIV.

118. Ibid, XXV.

119. Warren W. Wiersbe, *Be Joyful, NT Commentary, Philippians* (Colorado Springs: David C. Cook, 1974), 142.

120. Permission granted by Ruth Blandino to share her story on August 31, 2021.

Stephen Blandino

Stephen Blandino is the lead pastor of 7 City Church, an author, blogger, leadership coach, and host of the Leader Fluent Podcast. With over 20 years of experience in local church and nonprofit leadership, Stephen is passionate about helping people engage in personal growth, develop their full leadership capacity, and produce effective, Kingdom-advancing ministry. He holds a Master's in Organizational Leadership. Stephen lives in the Fort Worth, Texas, area with his wife Karen. They have one daughter, Ashley, son-in-law, Dylan, and two grandsons, Elijah and Wyatt.

Contact Stephen Blandino

Stephen Blandino blogs regularly at stephenblandino.com and is available to speak on a variety of topics. He has also written other books, and he offers leadership coaching opportunities and consulting. To learn more, or to contact Stephen, connect with him at:

Website: stephenblandino.com
Twitter: twitter.com/stephenblandino
Facebook: facebook.com/pastorstephenblandino
Instagram: Instagram.com/blandinostephen

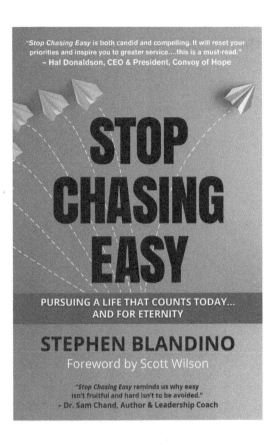

"*Stop Chasing Easy* is both candid and compelling. It will reset your priorities and inspire you to greater service....this is a must-read."
– Hal Donaldson, CEO & President, Convoy of Hope

STOP CHASING EASY

PURSUING A LIFE THAT COUNTS TODAY...
AND FOR ETERNITY

STEPHEN BLANDINO
Foreword by Scott Wilson

"*Stop Chasing Easy* reminds us why easy
isn't fruitful and hard isn't to be avoided."
– Dr. Sam Chand, Author & Leadership Coach

**Additional Resources Available at
Stephenblandino.com and
Stopchasingeasy.com**

**Masterclass for Leaders
Sermon Series Downloads
Small Group Discussion Guide**

Check out the Leader Fluent Podcast
with Stephen Blandino

Each episode equips leaders to create
thriving churches and organizations.

Subscribe Today on Your
Favorite Podcasting Platform